Arranged for *all* electronic keyboards *by Kenneth Baker.*

THE COMPLETE KEYBOARD PLAYER

CELINE DION

Wise Publications
London/New York/Paris/Sydney/Copenhagen/Madrid

Exclusive Distributors:
Music Sales Limited
8/9 Frith Street, London W1V 5TZ, England.
Music Sales Pty Limited
120 Rothschild Avenue, Rosebery, NSW 2018, Australia.

Order No. AM956274
ISBN 0-7119-7411-X

Compiled by Peter Evans
Music arranged by Kenneth Baker
Music processed by MSS Studios

Cover photograph courtesy of
London Features International

Printed in the United Kingdom by
Printwise (Haverhill) Limited, Suffolk.

I REMEMBER L.A.

Words & Music by Tony Colton & Richard Wold

Voice: clarinet
Rhythm: 8 beat
Tempo: medium (♩ = 100)

VERSES

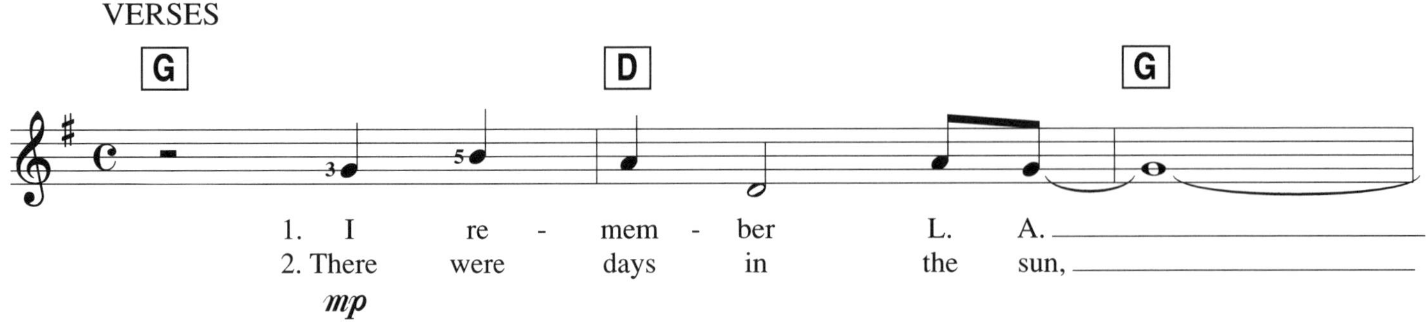

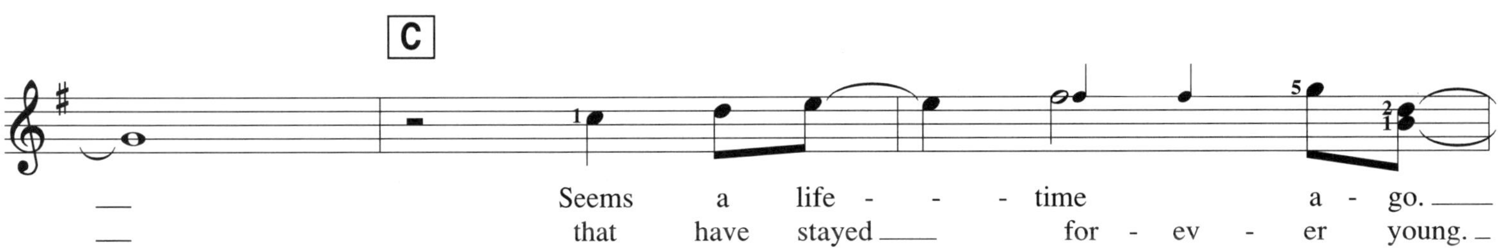

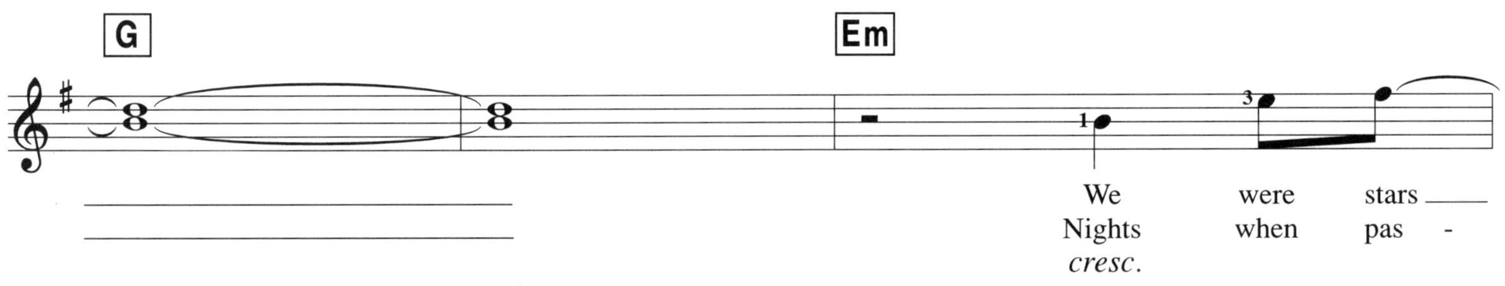

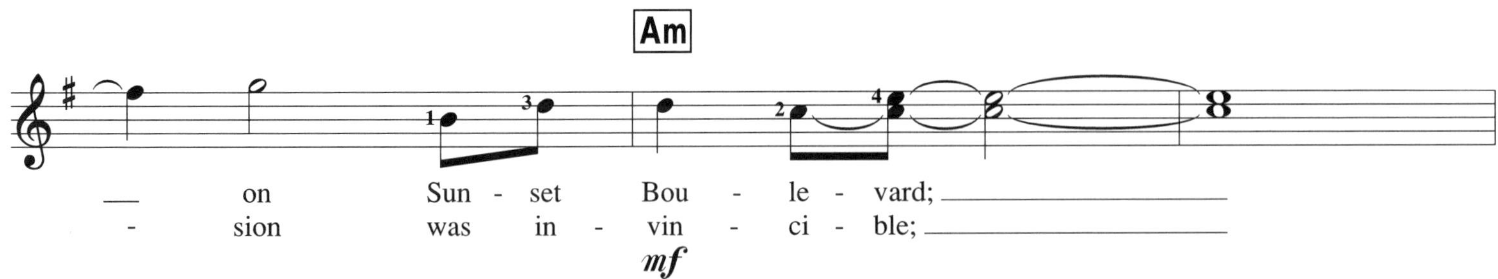

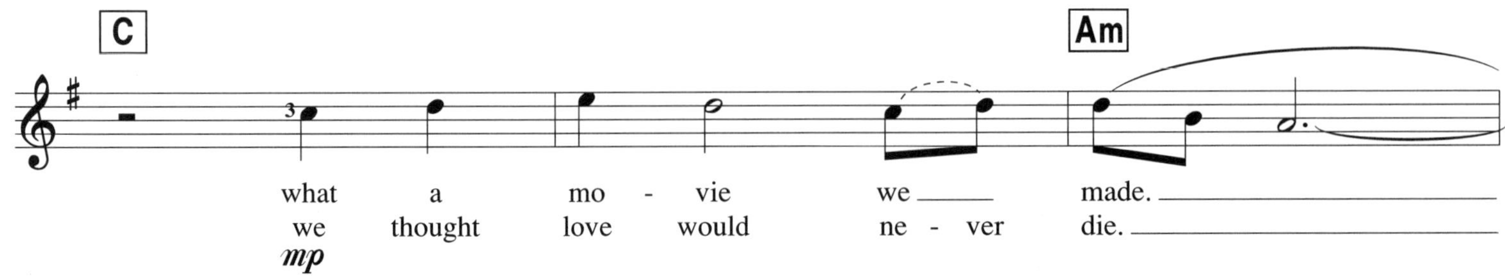

1.
2.
CHORUS
D7
D7
clarinet to piano
C
There were mo - ments in that life -
mf

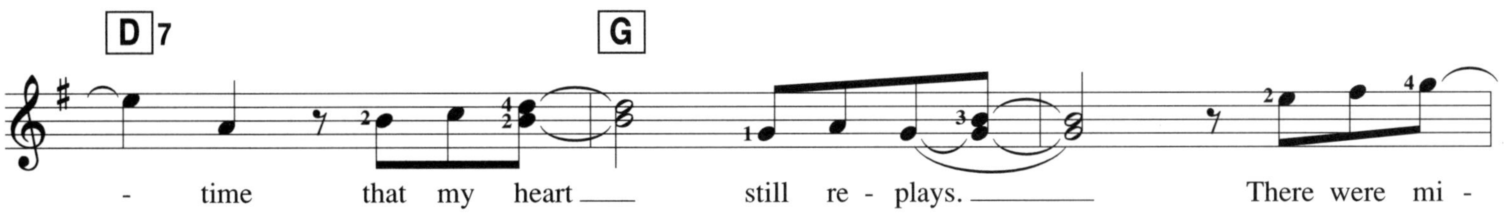

D7
G
- time that my heart still re - plays.
There were mi -

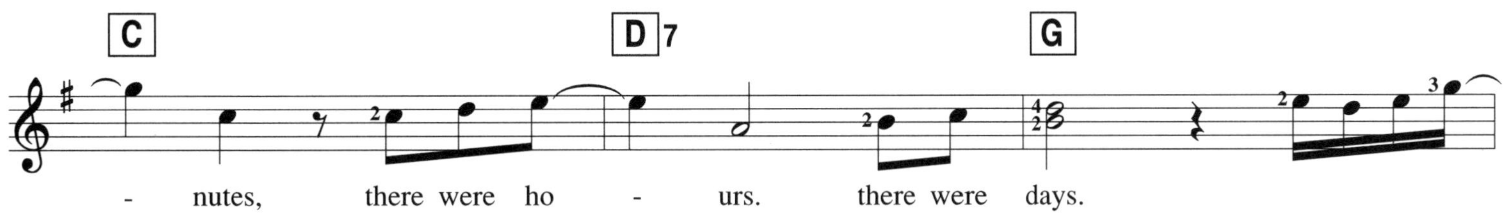

C
D7
G
- nutes, there were ho - urs. there were days.

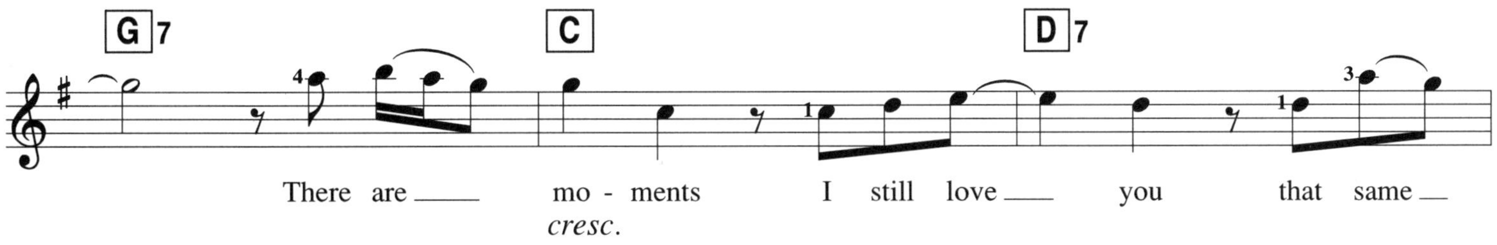

G7
C
D7
There are mo - ments I still love you that same
cresc.

Em
C
Am
way,
when I re -
f
dim.

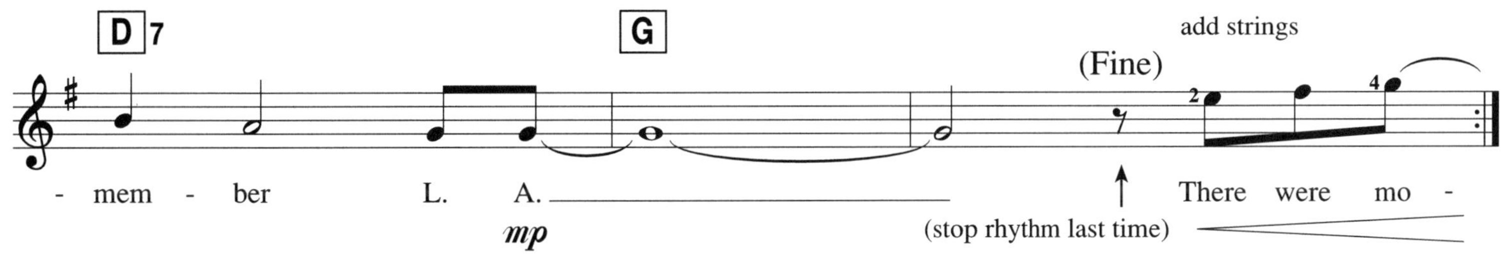

D7
G
add strings
(Fine)
- mem - ber L. A.
There were mo -
mp
(stop rhythm last time)

THINK TWICE

Words & Music by Andy Hill & Pete Sinfield

Voice: flute
Rhythm: 8 beat
Tempo: slow (♩ = 76)

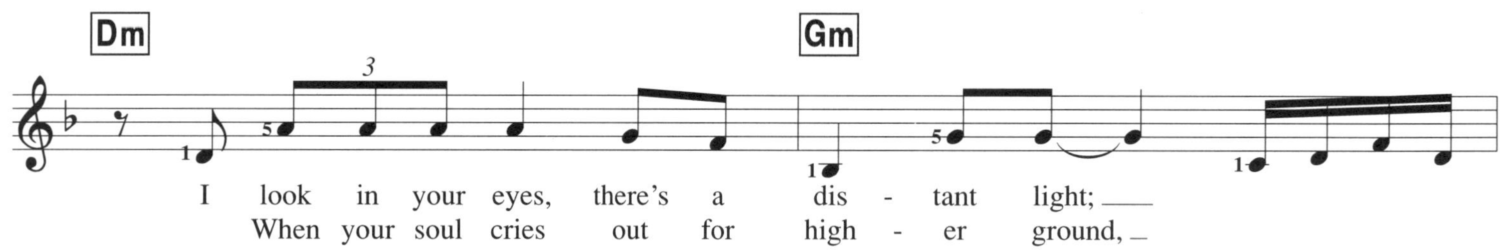

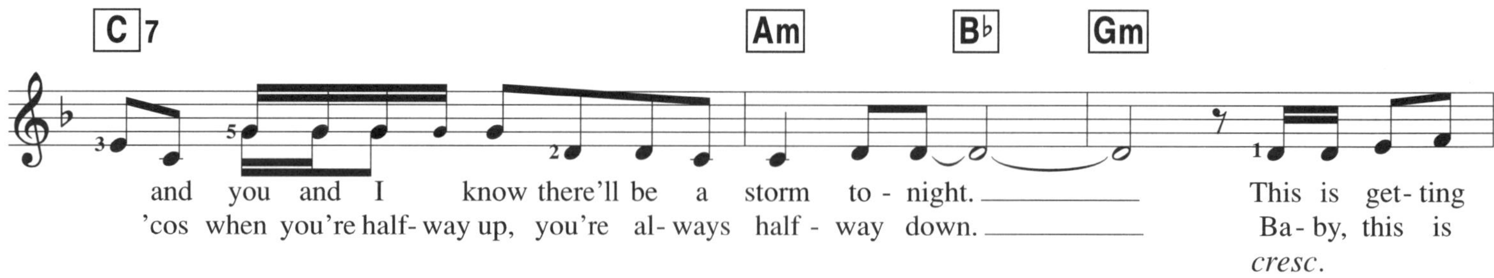

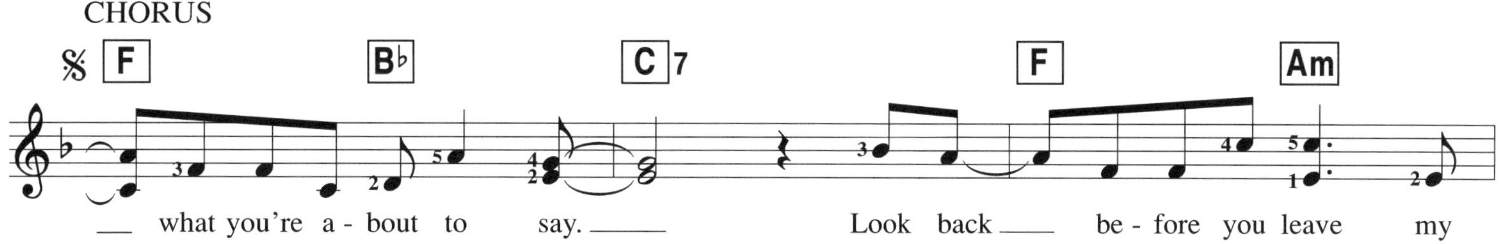
CHORUS
F
B♭
C7
F
Am
what you're a - bout to say.
Look back be - fore you leave my

B♭
C7
F
B♭
C7
life.
Be sure be - fore you close that door,
be - fore you

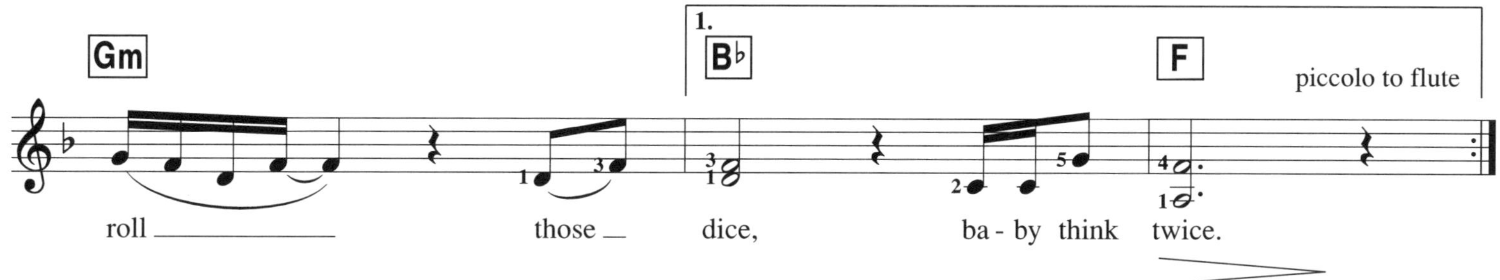
Gm
1.
B♭
F
piccolo to flute
roll those dice,
ba - by think twice.

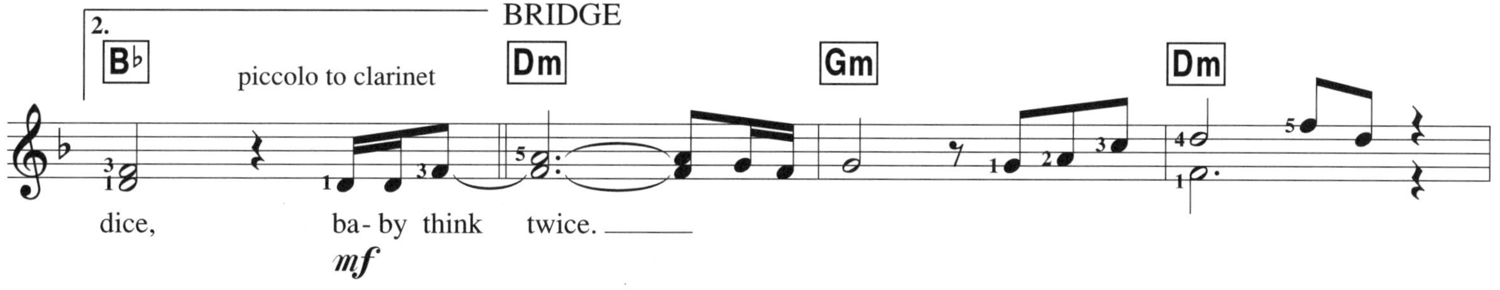
2.
B♭
piccolo to clarinet
BRIDGE
Dm
Gm
Dm
dice,
ba - by think twice.
mf

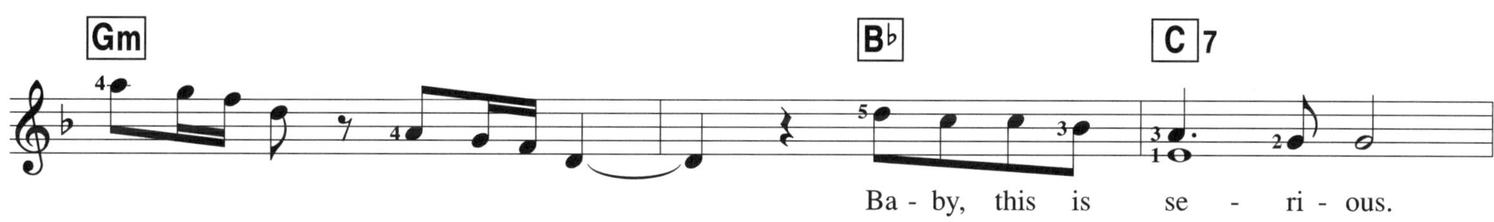
Gm
B♭
C7
Ba - by, this is se - ri - ous.

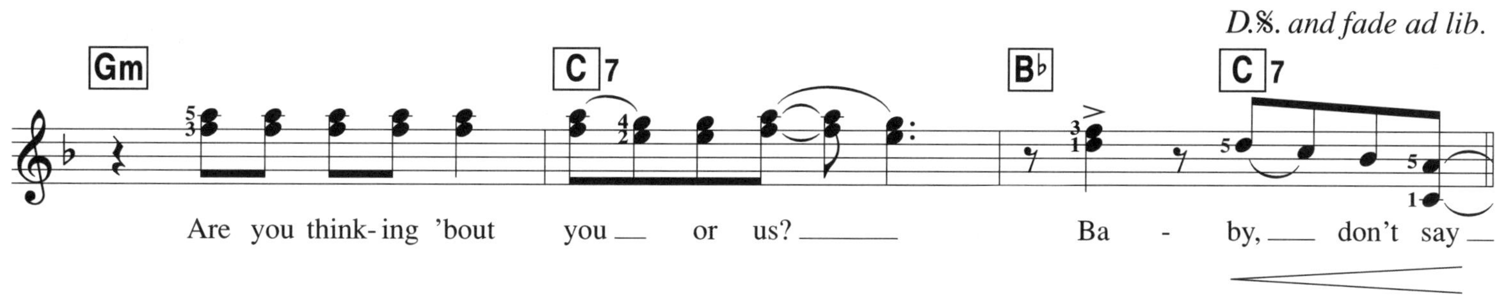
D.%. and fade ad lib.
Gm
C7
B♭
C7
Are you think - ing 'bout you or us?
Ba - by, don't say

I DON'T KNOW

Music by J. Kapler. Words by Jean Goldman & Philip Galdston

Voice: guitar
Rhythm: slow rock
Tempo: slow (♩. = 60)

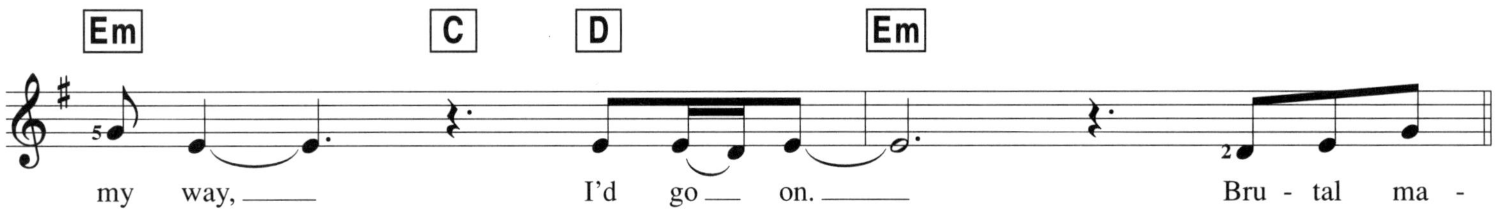

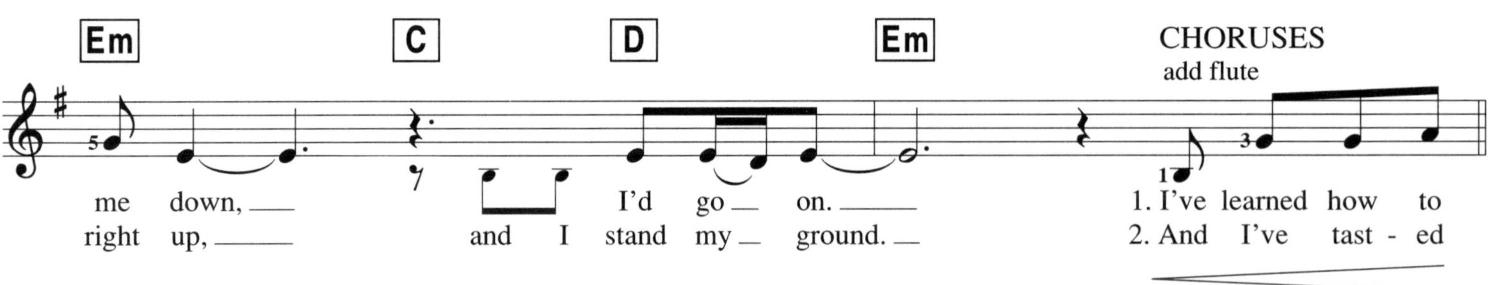

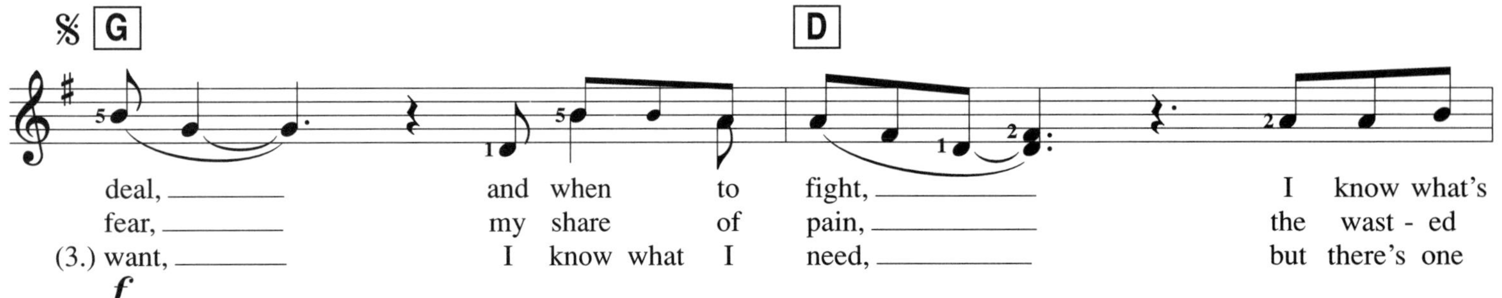

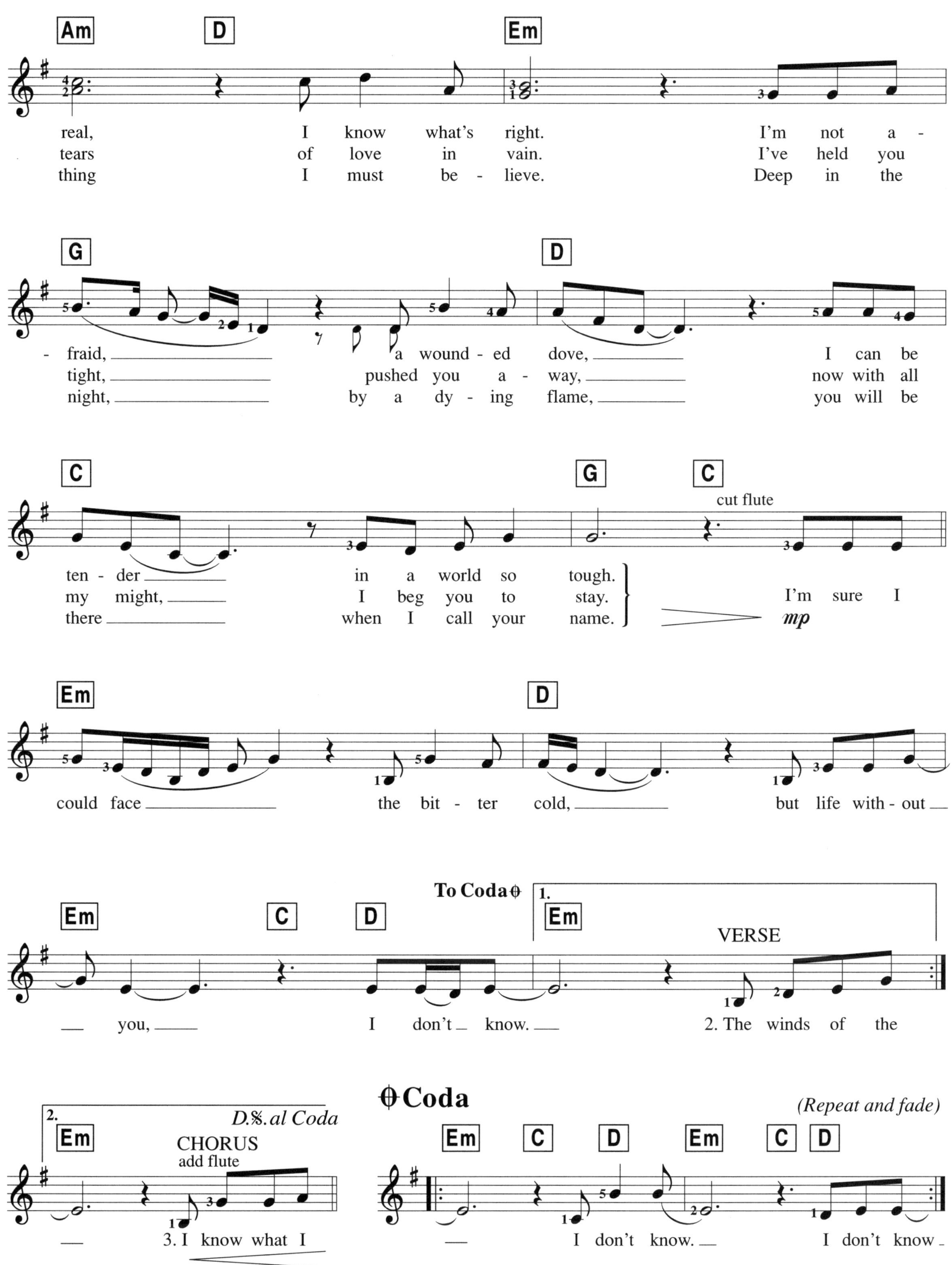
Am
D
Em
real, I know what's right. I'm not a -
tears of love in vain. I've held you
thing I must be - lieve. Deep in the
G
D
- fraid, a wound - ed dove, I can be
tight, pushed you a - way, now with all
night, by a dy - ing flame, you will be
C
G
C
cut flute
ten - der in a world so tough.
my might, I beg you to stay.
there when I call your name.
I'm sure I
mp
Em
D
could face the bit - ter cold, but life with - out
To Coda
1.
Em
C
D
Em
VERSE
you, I don't know.
2. The winds of the
2.
D.%. al Coda
Em
CHORUS
add flute
3. I know what I
Coda
(Repeat and fade)
Em
C
D
Em
C
D
I don't know. I don't know

THE POWER OF LOVE

Words & Music by C. deRouge, G. Mende, J. Rush & S. Applegate

Voice: piano
Rhythm: 8 beat
Tempo: slow (♩ = 72)

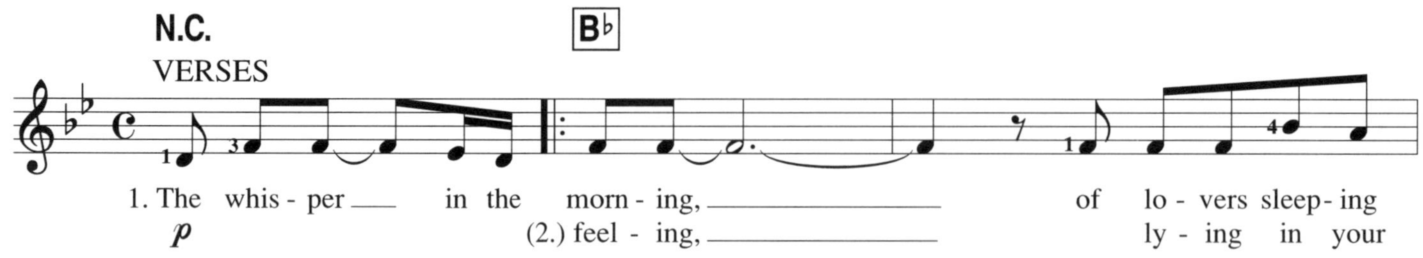

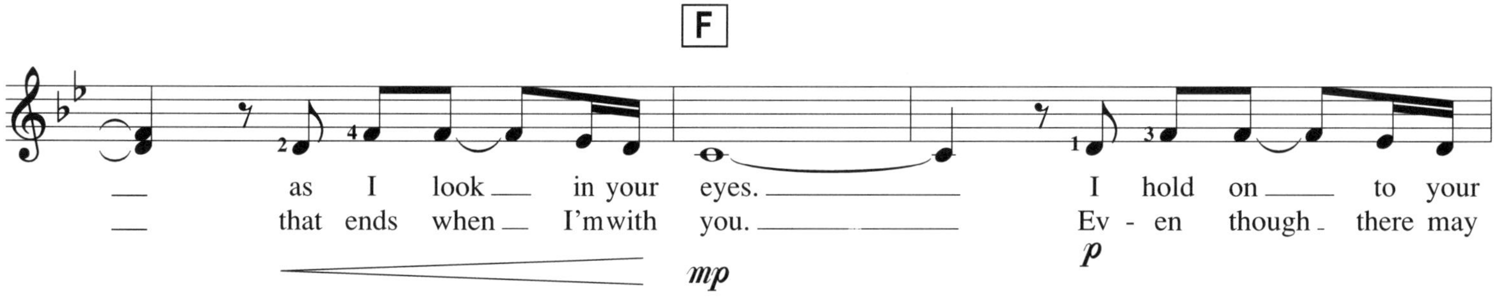

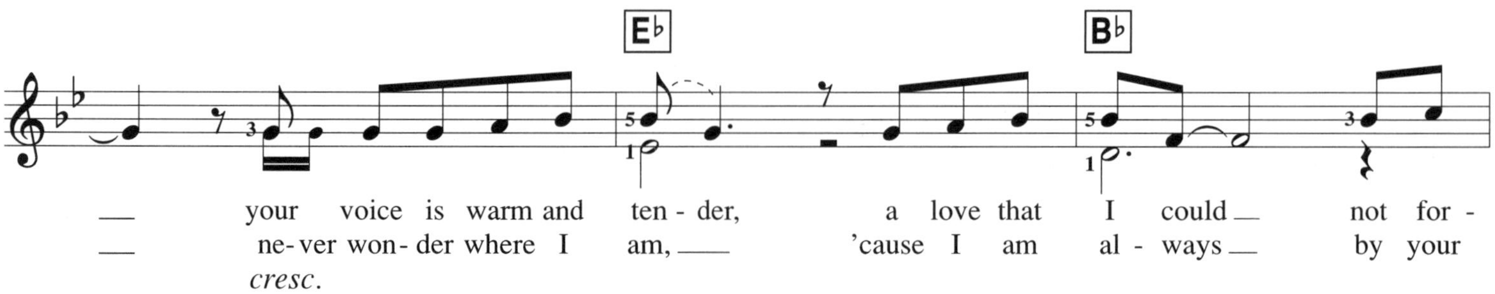

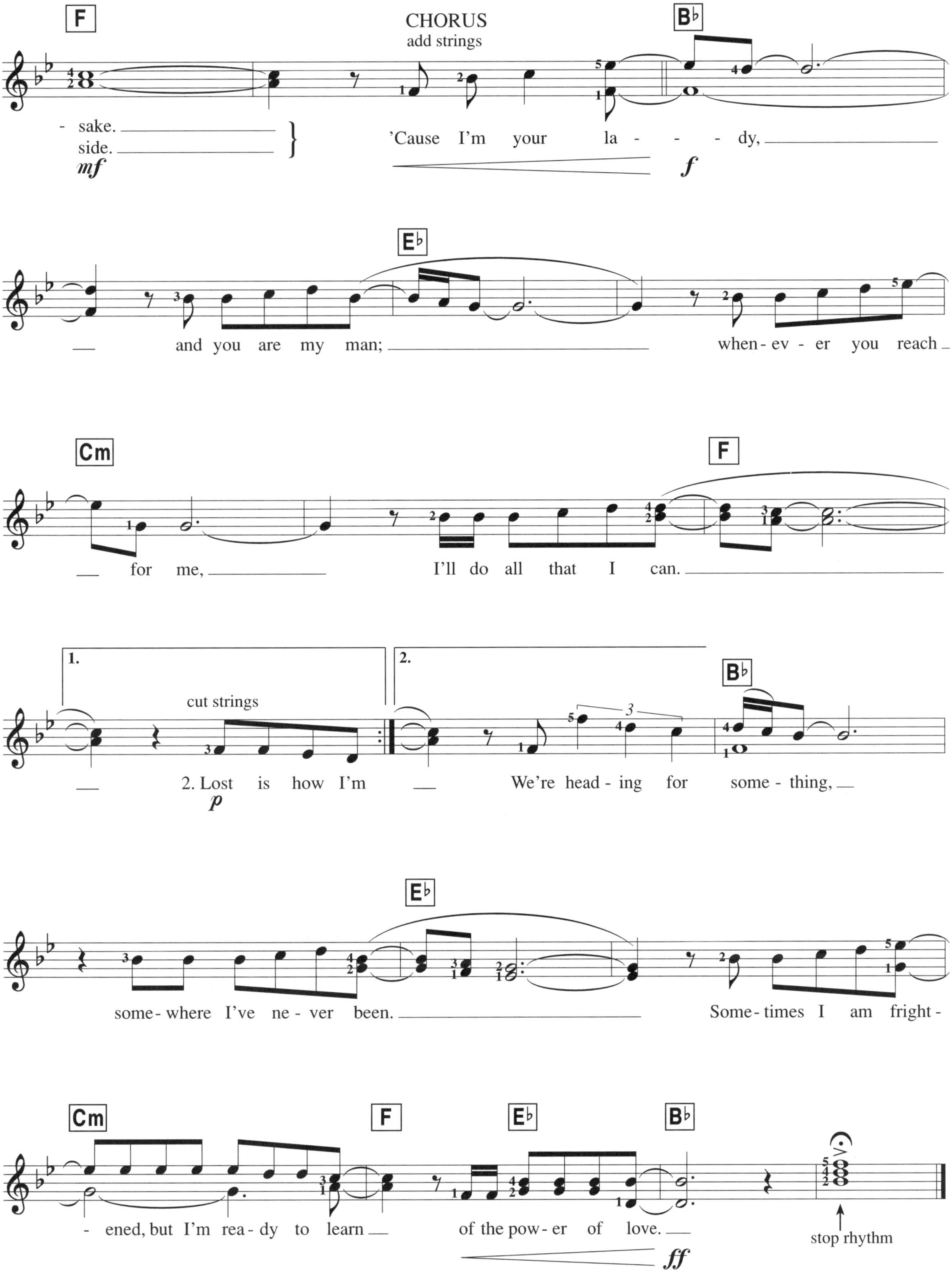

F

CHORUS
add strings

B♭

- sake. ______
side. ______
mf

'Cause I'm your la - - - dy, ______
f

E♭

___ and you are my man; ______ when-ev-er you reach ___

Cm

F

___ for me, ______ I'll do all that I can. ______

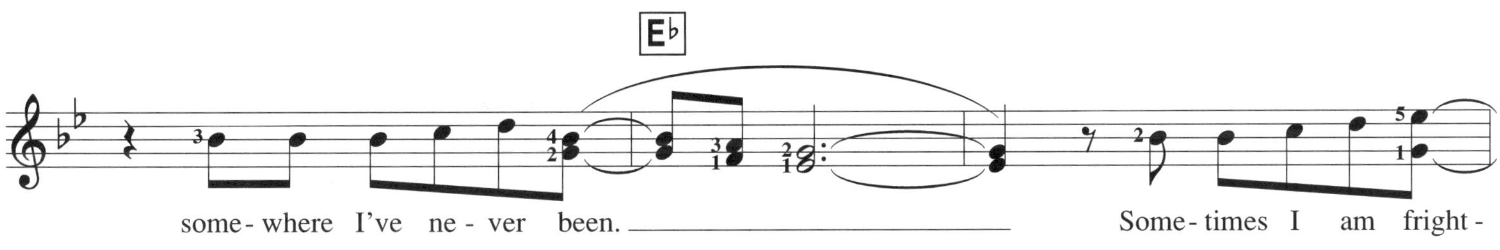

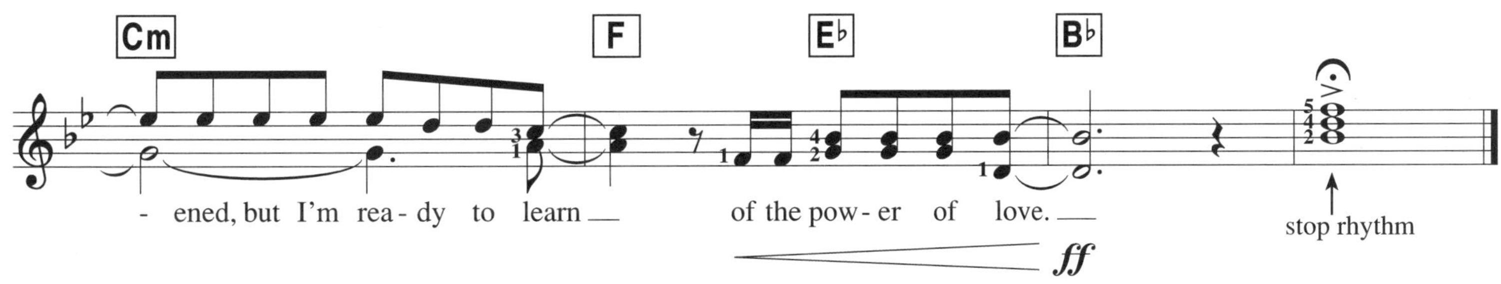

MISLED

Words & Music by Peter Zizzo & Jimmy Bralower

Voice: tenor sax.

Rhythm: rock

Tempo: medium (♩ = 112)

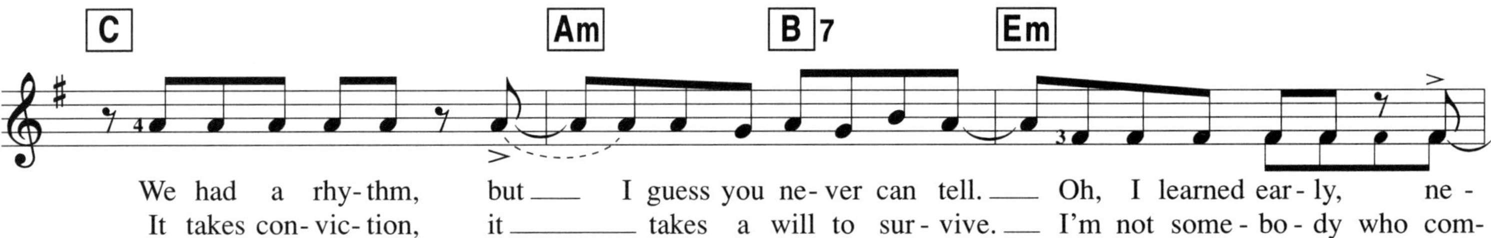

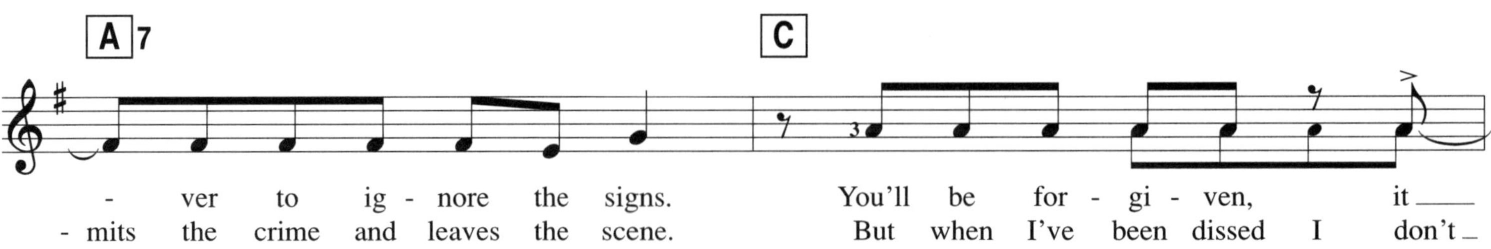

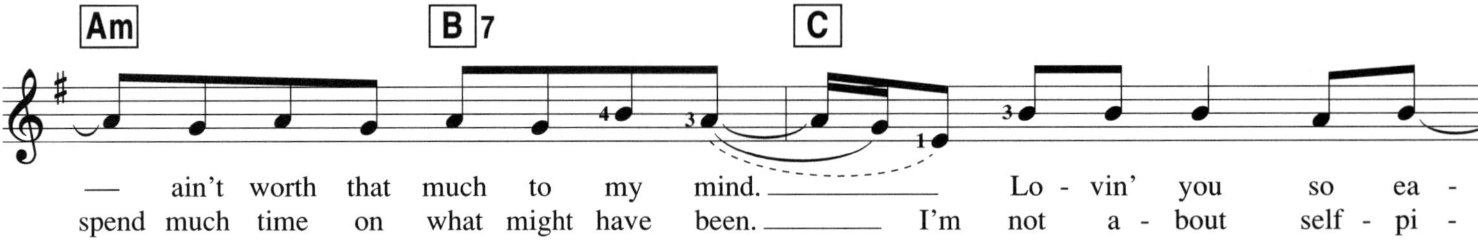

G
D
Em
- sy, it's hard to say good-bye, but if that's the way it goes, it goes.
- ty, your love did me wrong. Now I'm mo-ving, mo-ving on.
CHORUS
Am
B7
Em
Am
B7
Just a page in my his - to-ry; just an-oth-er one of those mys-
f

Em
Am
B7
Em
- te-ries. One more lo-ver that used to be, if you

Am
B7
Em
INSTRUMENTAL
sax to brass
A7
think you're in my head, you been se-ri-ous-ly mis-led!
mf

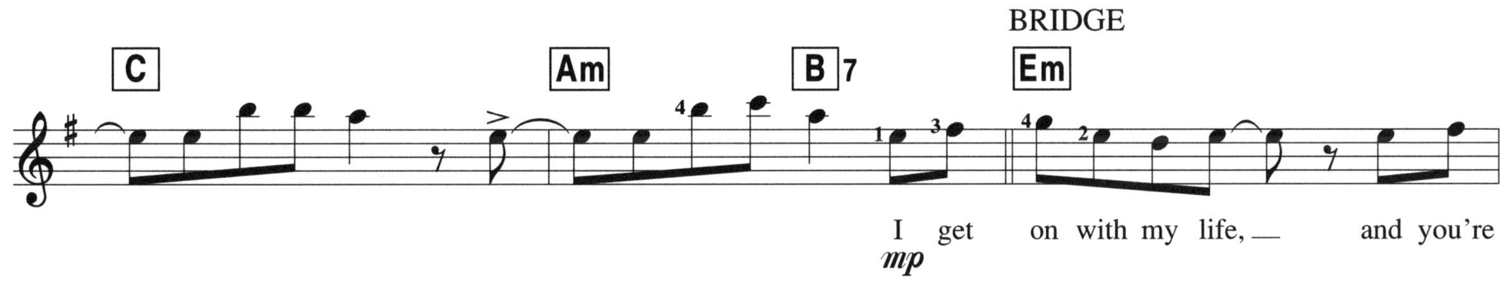
C
Am
B7
BRIDGE
Em
I get on with my life, and you're
mp

D.%. (fade ad lib.)
A7
C
Am
B7
brass to sax.
not on my mind, and I took half the time to get ov - er you.

JUST WALK AWAY

Words & Music by Albert Hammond & Marti Sharron

Voice: oboe
Rhythm: 8 beat
Tempo: slow (♩ = 76)

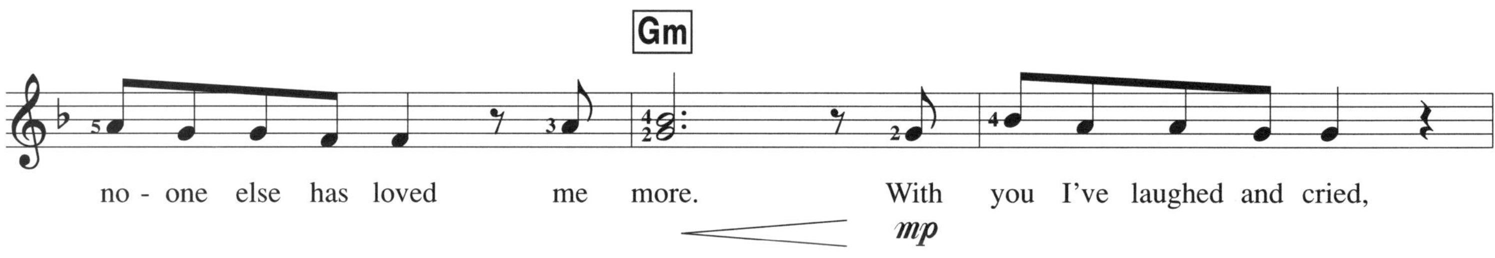

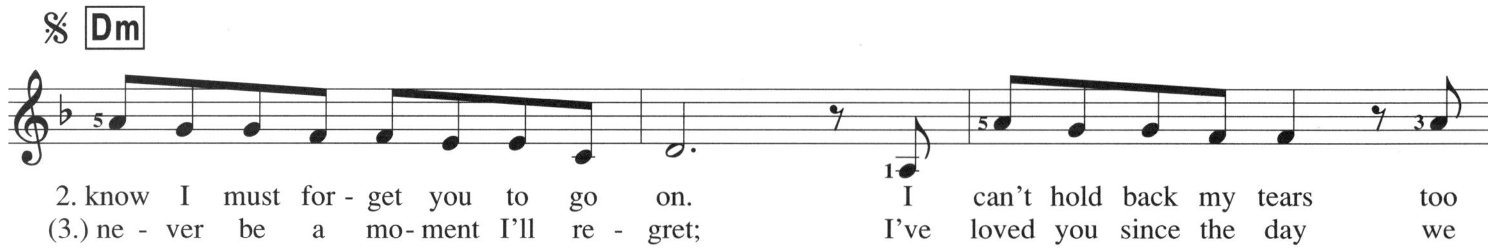

B♭7
A7
Dm
CHORUS
clarinet to strings
Gm
find the strength I need to let you go.
know I've got to find the strength to say:
Just walk a - way, just say good -
f
C7
F
B♭
- bye. Don't turn a - round now, you may see me cry. I
mf
Gm
B♭m
Dm
must - n't fall a - part, or show my bro - ken heart, or the love I feel for
D7
Gm
C7
you. So walk a - way, and close the door, and let my
f
F
B♭
E♭
life be as it was be - fore. And I'll ne - ver, ne - ver know just
Dm
B♭7
A7
Dm
strings to clarinet
(Fine)
D.𝄋 al Fine
how I let you go, but there's no - thing left to say, just walk a - way. 3. There'll
(stop rhythm last time)
p

SEDUCES ME

Music by Dan Hill & John Shead. Words by Dan Hill

Voice: clarinet
Rhythm: slow rock
Tempo: medium (♩. = 69)

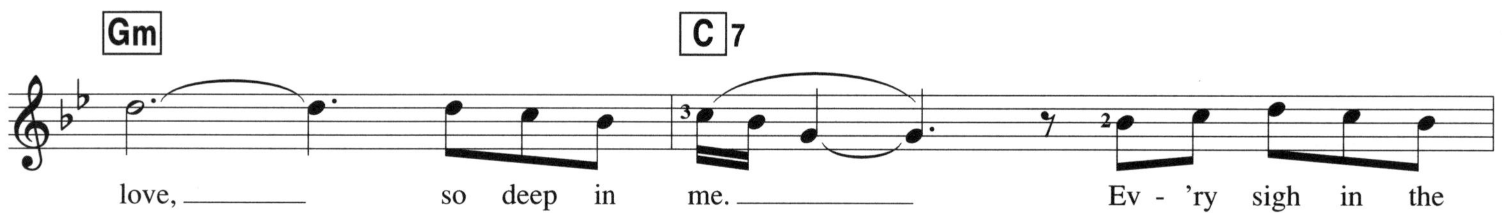

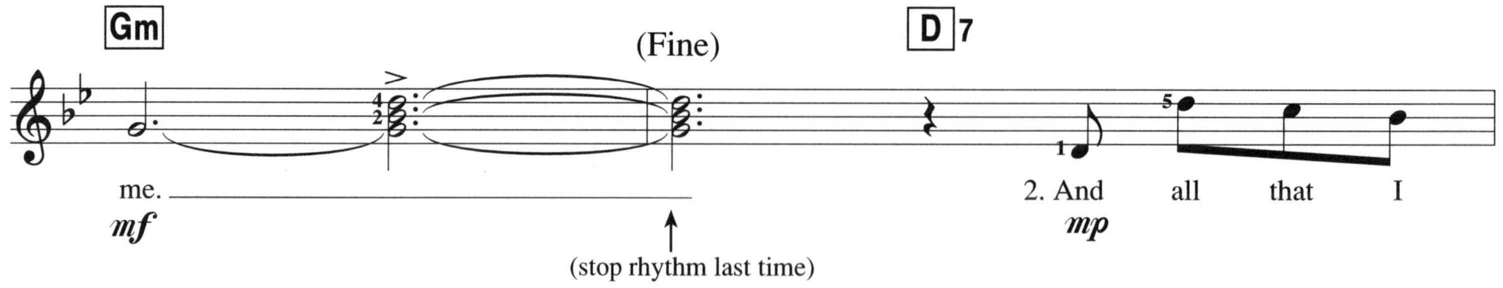

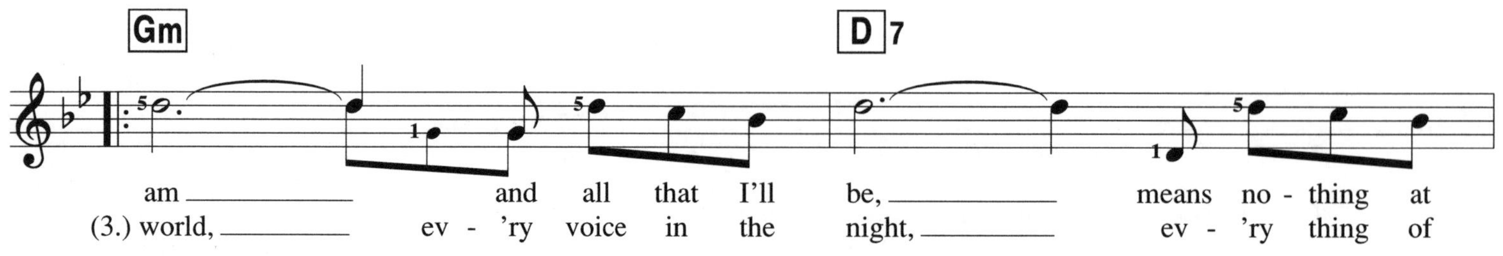

Gm
C7
all, if you can't be with me. Your most in-no-cent
beau-ty comes shi-ning through your eyes. And all that is

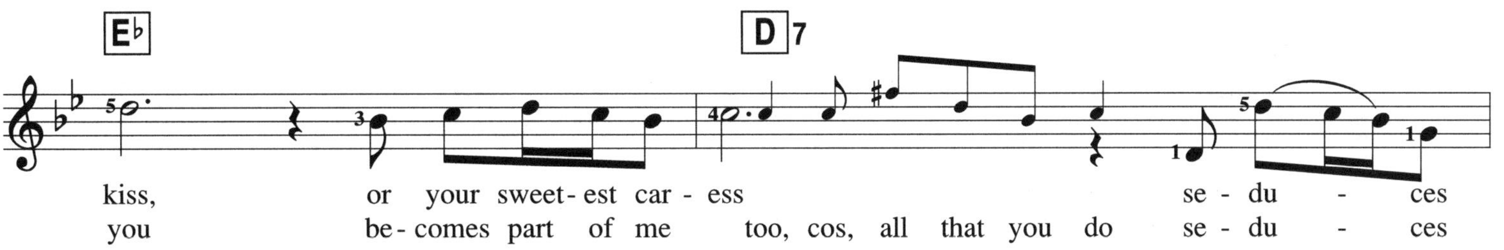
E♭
D7
kiss, or your sweet-est car-ess se-du-ces
you be-comes part of me too, cos, all that you do se-du-ces

BRIDGE
Gm
D7
Gm
clarinet to horn
me. I don't care a-bout to-mor-row,
me. And if I should die to-mor-row,
mf

D7
Gm
B♭
A7
I've gi-ven up on yes-ter-day. Here and now is all that
I'd go down with a smile on my face. I thank God I've ev-er

Dm
E7
mat-ters, be-cause right here with you is where I'll
known you, I fall down on my knees for all the

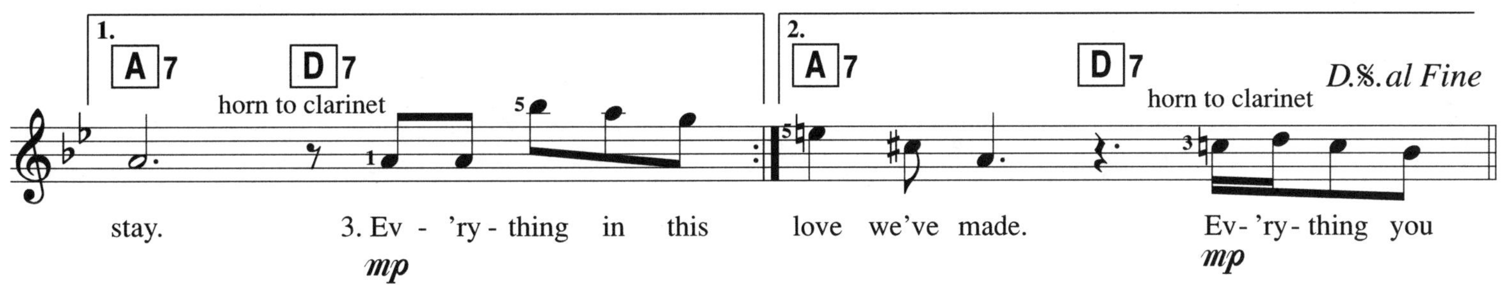
1.
2.
A7
D7
horn to clarinet
A7
D7
horn to clarinet
D.%. al Fine
stay. 3. Ev-'ry-thing in this love we've made. Ev-'ry-thing you
mp
mp

LET'S TALK ABOUT LOVE

Words & Music by Bryan Adams, Eliot Kennedy & Jean-Jacques Goldman

Voice: flute
Rhythm: 8 beat
Tempo: slow (♩ = 68)

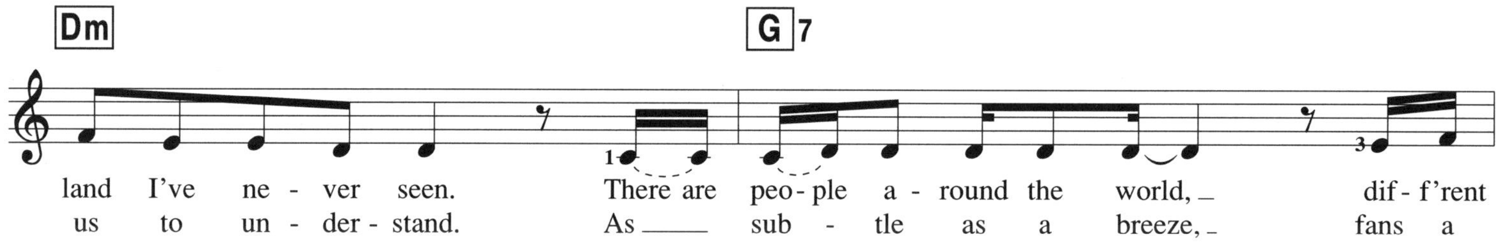

G7
C
G7
VERSE
C
guitar to flute
trust. Lets talk a - bout love. 3. It's the king of all who live, and the
mp

Am
F
Dm
queen of all good hearts. It's the ace you may keep up your sleeve, till the game is all but lost. Ooh, as

G7
C
F
Dm
deep as a - ny sea, with the rage of a - ny storm. But as gen - tle as a fal - ling leaf on

G7
CHORUS
flute to guitar
C
Am
a - ny au - tumn morn. Let's talk a - bout love, let's talk a - bout us. Let's talk a - bout
f

Dm
G7
C
life, let's talk a - bout trust. Let's talk a - bout love, let's talk a - bout

Am
Dm
G7
(Repeat and fade)
us. Let's talk a - bout life, let's talk a - bout trust. Let's talk a - bout

MY HEART WILL GO ON (Love Theme from 'Titanic')

Words & Music by James Horner & Will Jennings

Voice: alto saxophone
Rhythm: 8 beat
Tempo: medium (♩ = 100)

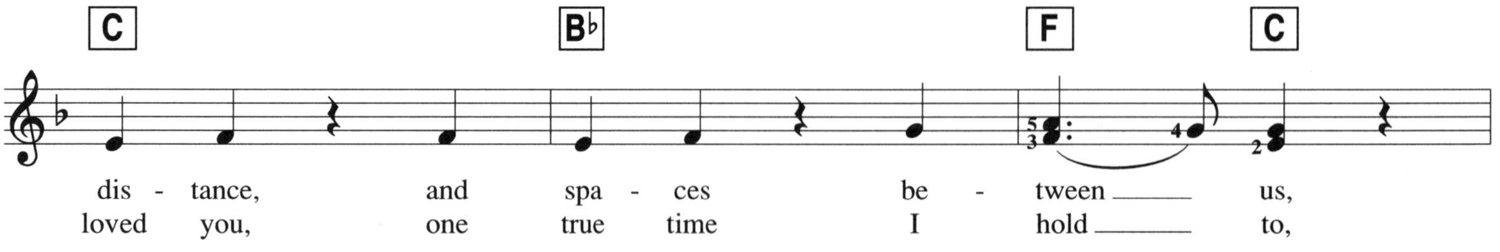

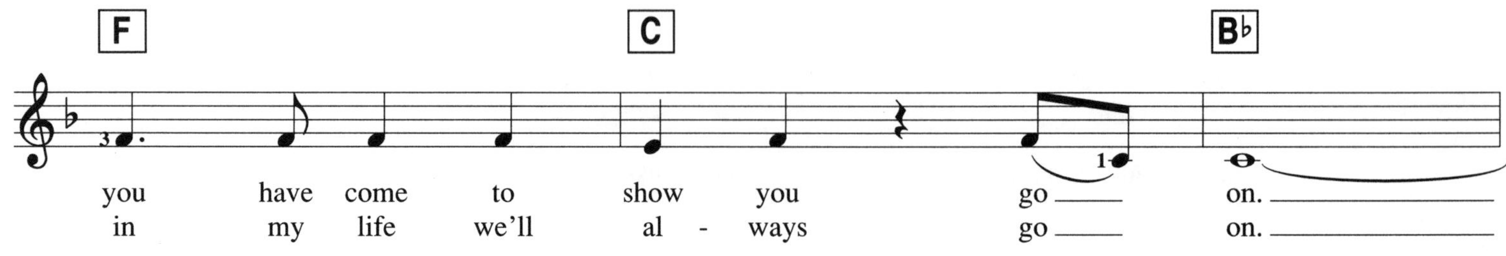

CHORUS
C
A7
add strings
Dm
C
Near,
far,
where -
mf
B♭
C
Dm
- ev - er you are,
I be - lieve that the
f
C
B♭
Am
Gm
Dm
heart does go on.
Once
mf
C
B♭
C
more you op - en the door,
and you're
f
Dm
Am
B♭
here in my heart, and my heart will go
1.
F
C
F
cut strings
on and on.
2.
F
C
molto rit.
F
on and on.
stop rhythm

THE LAST TO KNOW

Words & Music by Philip Galdston & Brock Walsh

Voice: guitar
Rhythm: 8 beat
Tempo: slow (♩ = 75)

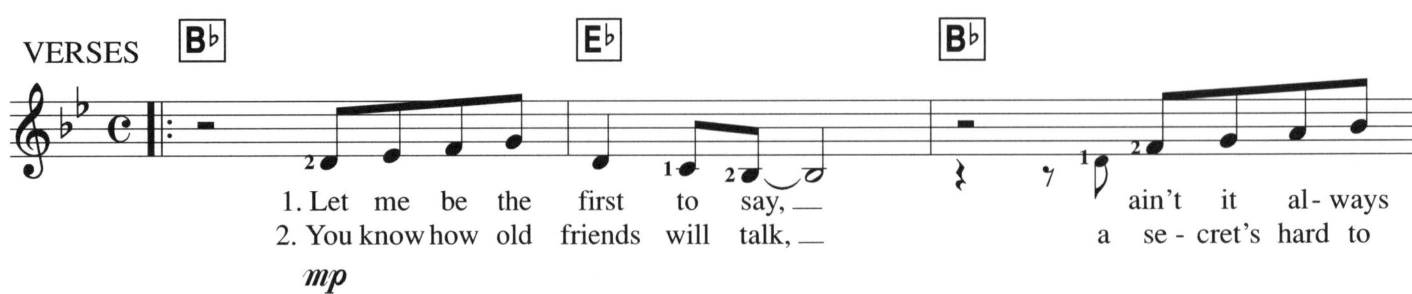

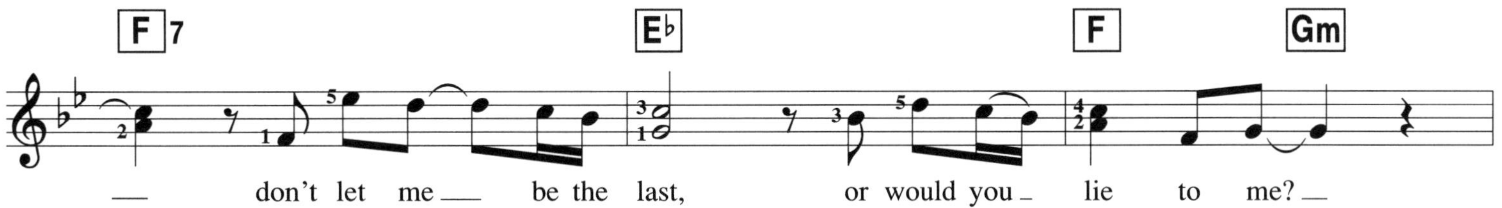
F7
E♭
F
Gm
don't let me be the last, or would you lie to me?

E♭
F
Don't you keep it to your-self for my pro - tec - tion, break it to me
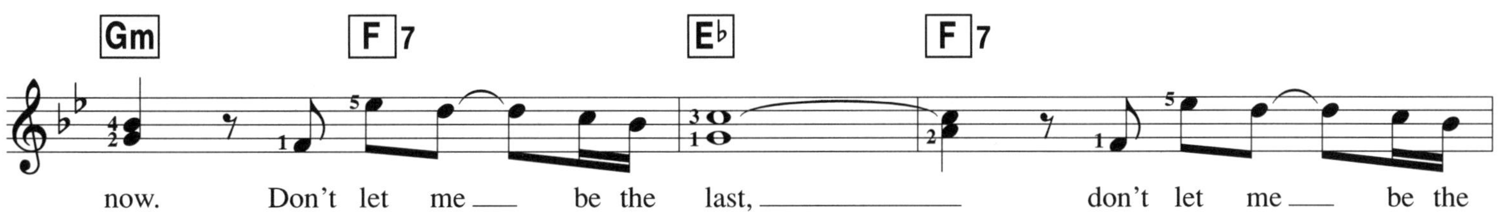
Gm
F7
E♭
F7
now. Don't let me be the last, don't let me be the

E♭
Gm
E♭
last, or would you lie to me? Ba - by, all I ask, don't

Cm
F7
1.
B♭
cut flute
Cm
F7
let me be the last to know.

2.
G♭
D♭
E
G♭
D♭
F7
D.%. Repeat CHORUS and fade
Don't let me be the

IT'S ALL COMING BACK TO ME NOW

Words & Music by Jim Steinman

Voice: flute
Rhythm: 8 beat
Tempo: medium (♩ = 92)

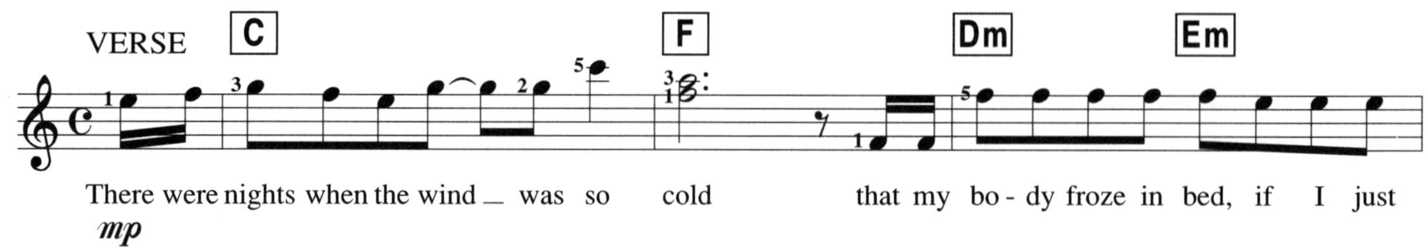

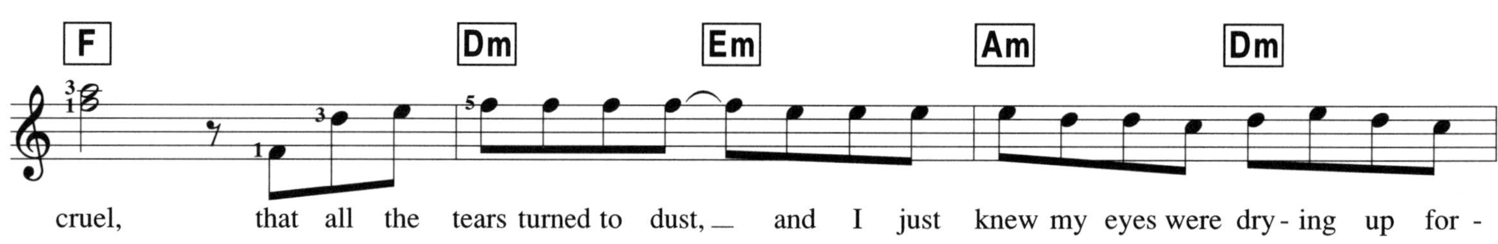

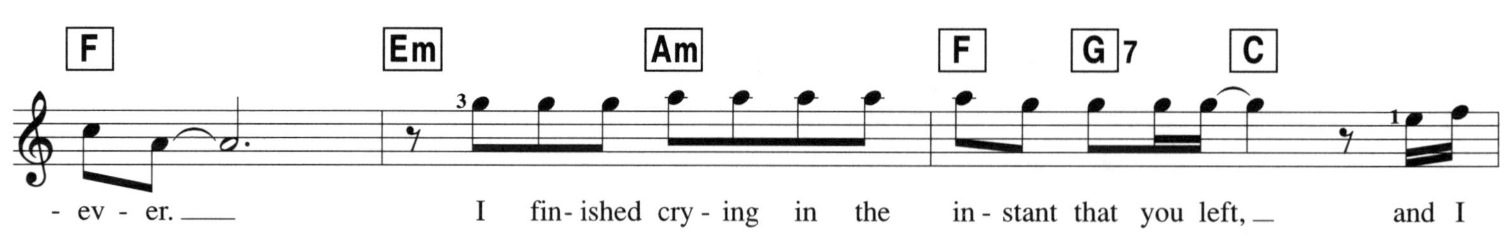

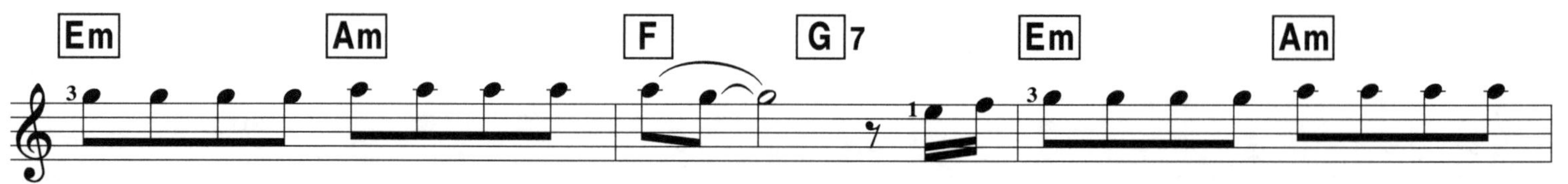

CHORUS
F
G7
F
G7
flute to brass ensemble
C
Em
I had ev-er made.
But when you touch me like this, and you hold me like that, I just
f
kiss you like this, if you whis-per like that, I was

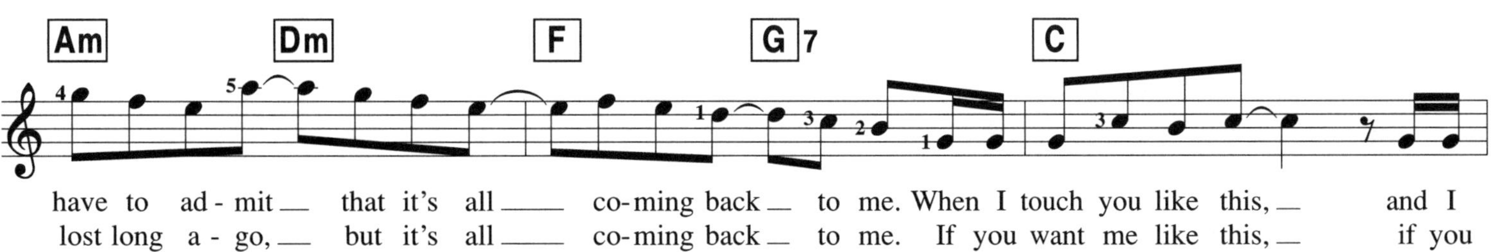
Am
Dm
F
G7
C
have to ad-mit that it's all co-ming back to me. When I touch you like this, and I
lost long a-go, but it's all co-ming back to me. If you want me like this, if you

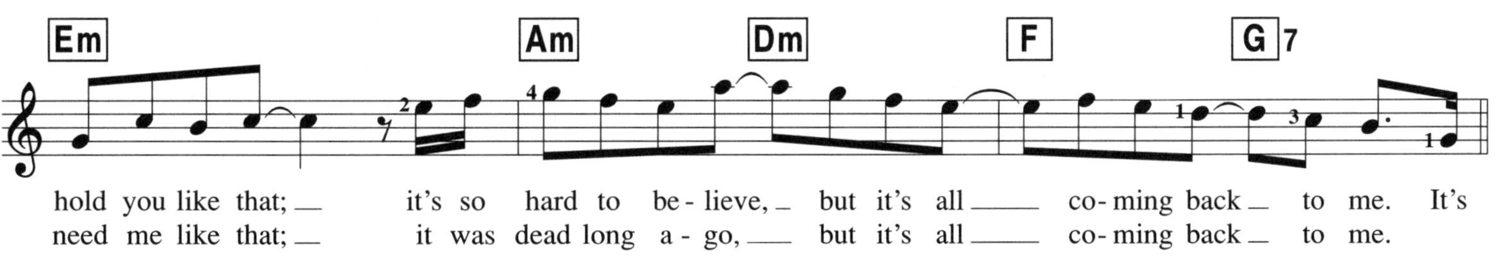
Em
Am
Dm
F
G7
hold you like that; it's so hard to be-lieve, but it's all co-ming back to me. It's
need me like that; it was dead long a-go, but it's all co-ming back to me.

BRIDGE
C
F
Em
F
all co-ming back, it's all co-ming back to me now. There were mo-ments of gold, and there were

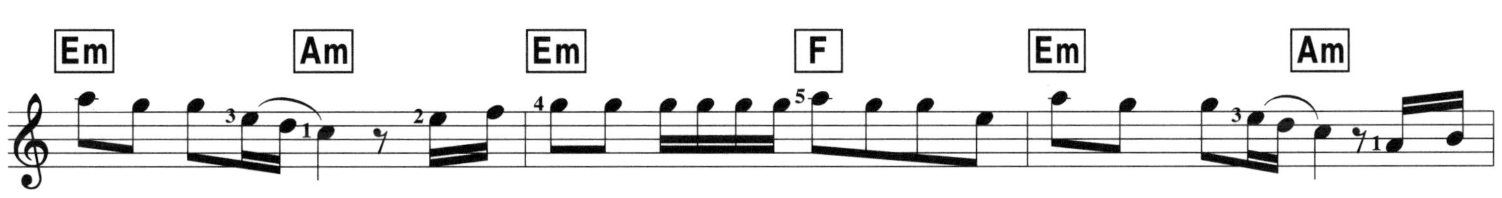
Em
Am
Em
F
Em
Am
flash-es of light. There were things I'd ne-ver do a-gain, but then, they'd al-ways seemed right. There were

D.S. Repeat 1st 8 bars of CHORUS and fade for ending
F
G7
nights of end-less plea-sure, it was more than a-ny laws al-low. Ba-by. ba-by, if I

ALL BY MYSELF

Words & Music by Eric Carmen

Voice: piano solo
Rhythm: 8 beat
Tempo: slow (♩ = 62)

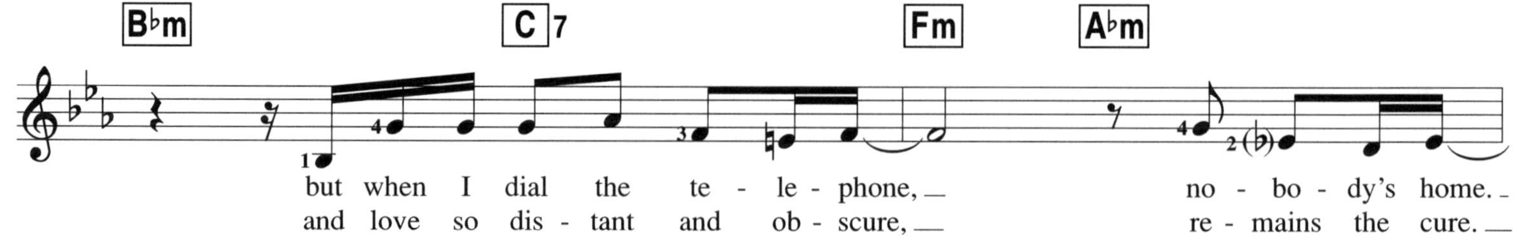

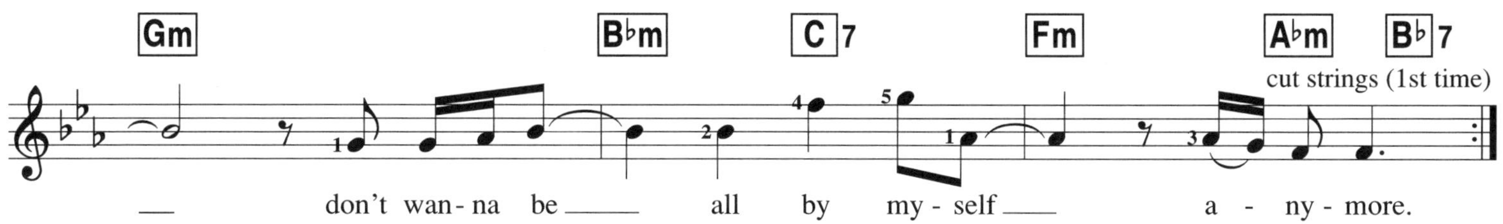
Gm
B♭m
C7
Fm
A♭m
B♭7
cut strings (1st time)
don't wan-na be all by my-self a-ny-more.
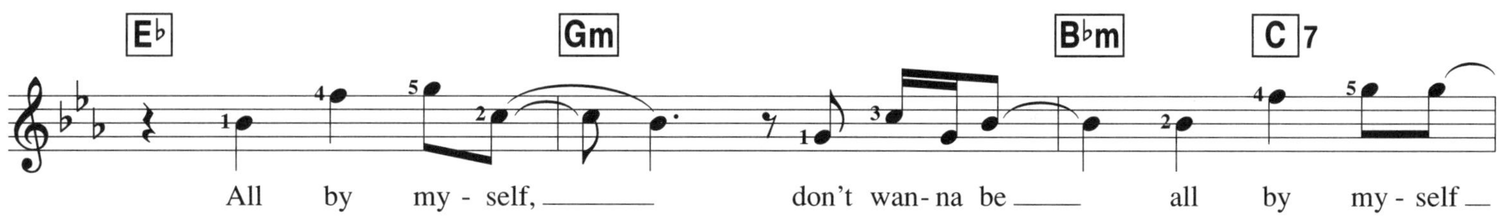
E♭
Gm
B♭m
C7
All by my-self, don't wan-na be all by my-self
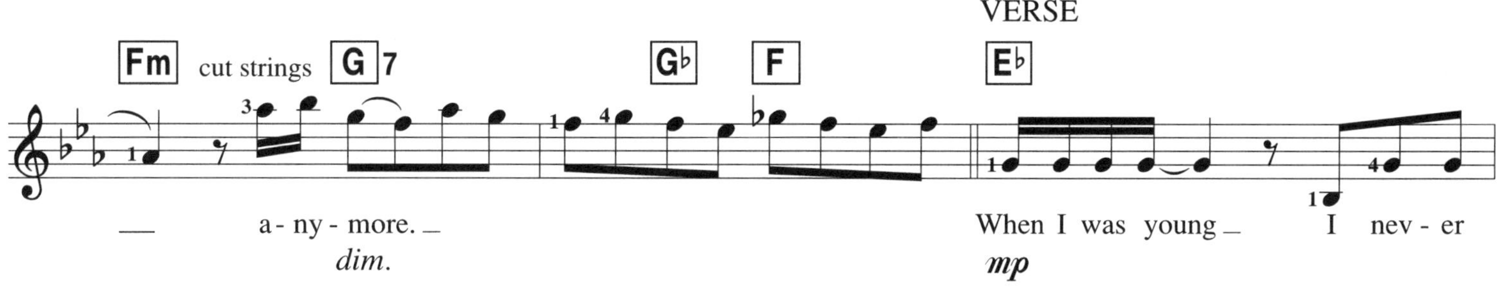
VERSE
Fm
cut strings
G7
G♭
F
E♭
a-ny-more.
dim.
When I was young I nev-er
mp
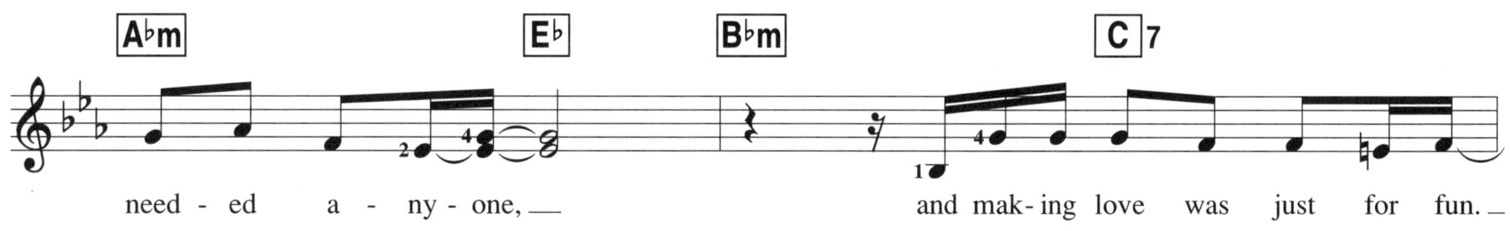
A♭m
E♭
B♭m
C7
need-ed a-ny-one,
and mak-ing love was just for fun.
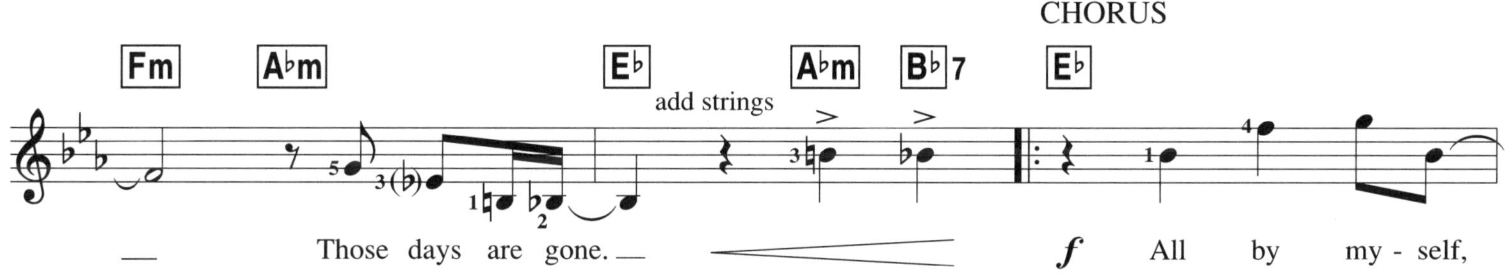
CHORUS
Fm
A♭m
E♭
A♭m
B♭7
E♭
add strings
Those days are gone.
f
All by my-self,
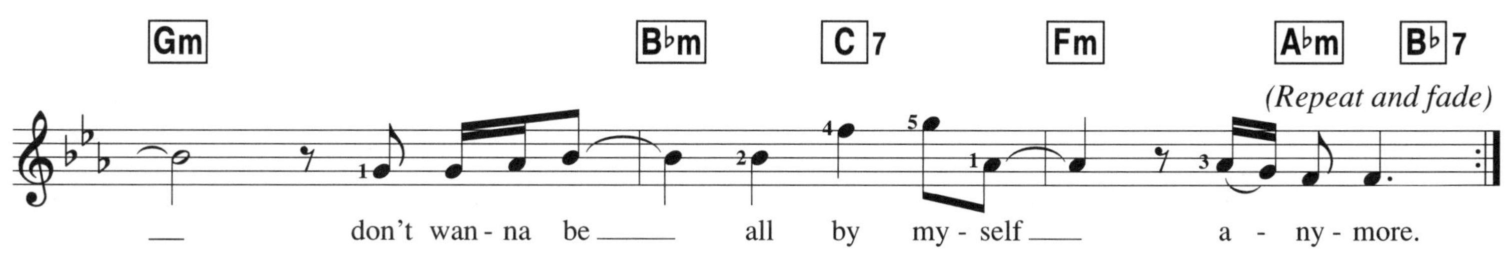
Gm
B♭m
C7
Fm
A♭m
B♭7
(Repeat and fade)
don't wan-na be all by my-self a-ny-more.

LOVE DOESN'T ASK WHY

Words & Music by Philip Galdston, Barry Mann & Cynthia Weil

Voice: brass ensemble
Rhythm: 8 beat
Tempo: slow (♩ = 76)

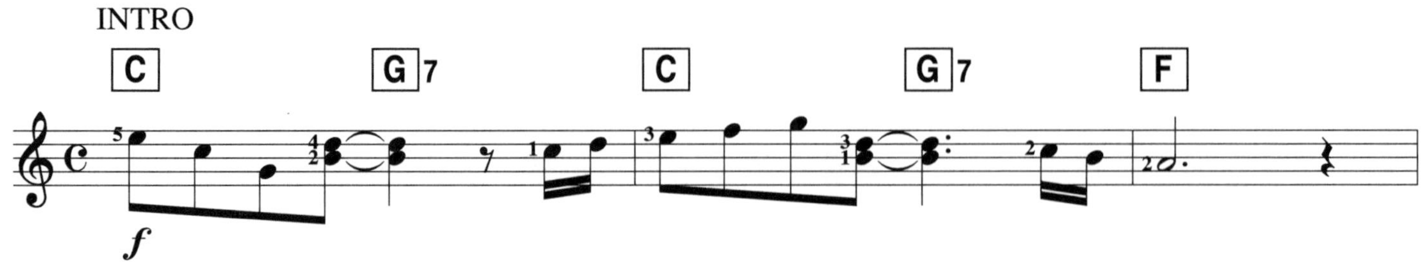

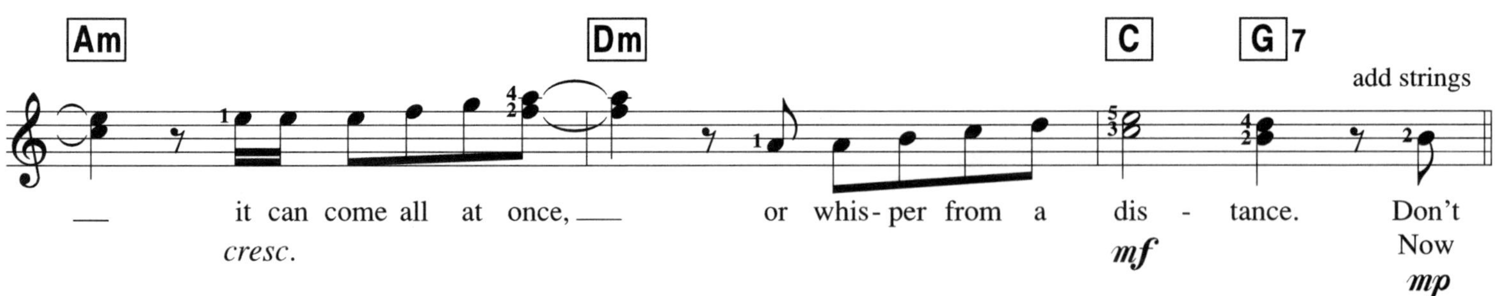

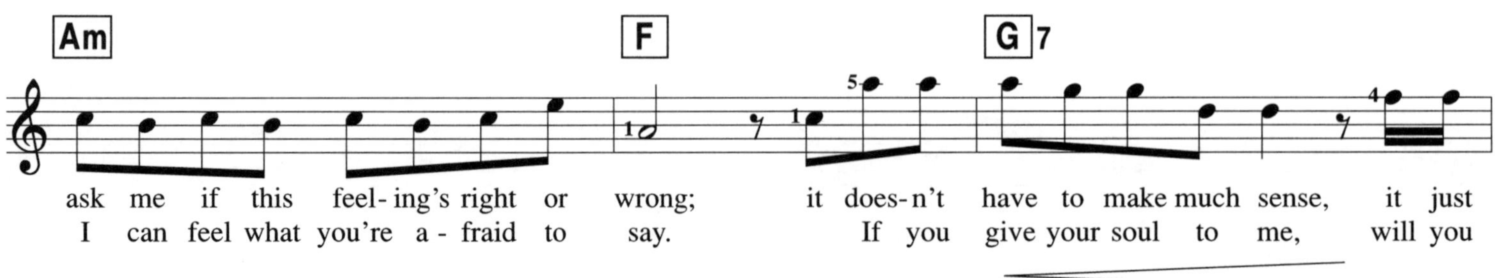

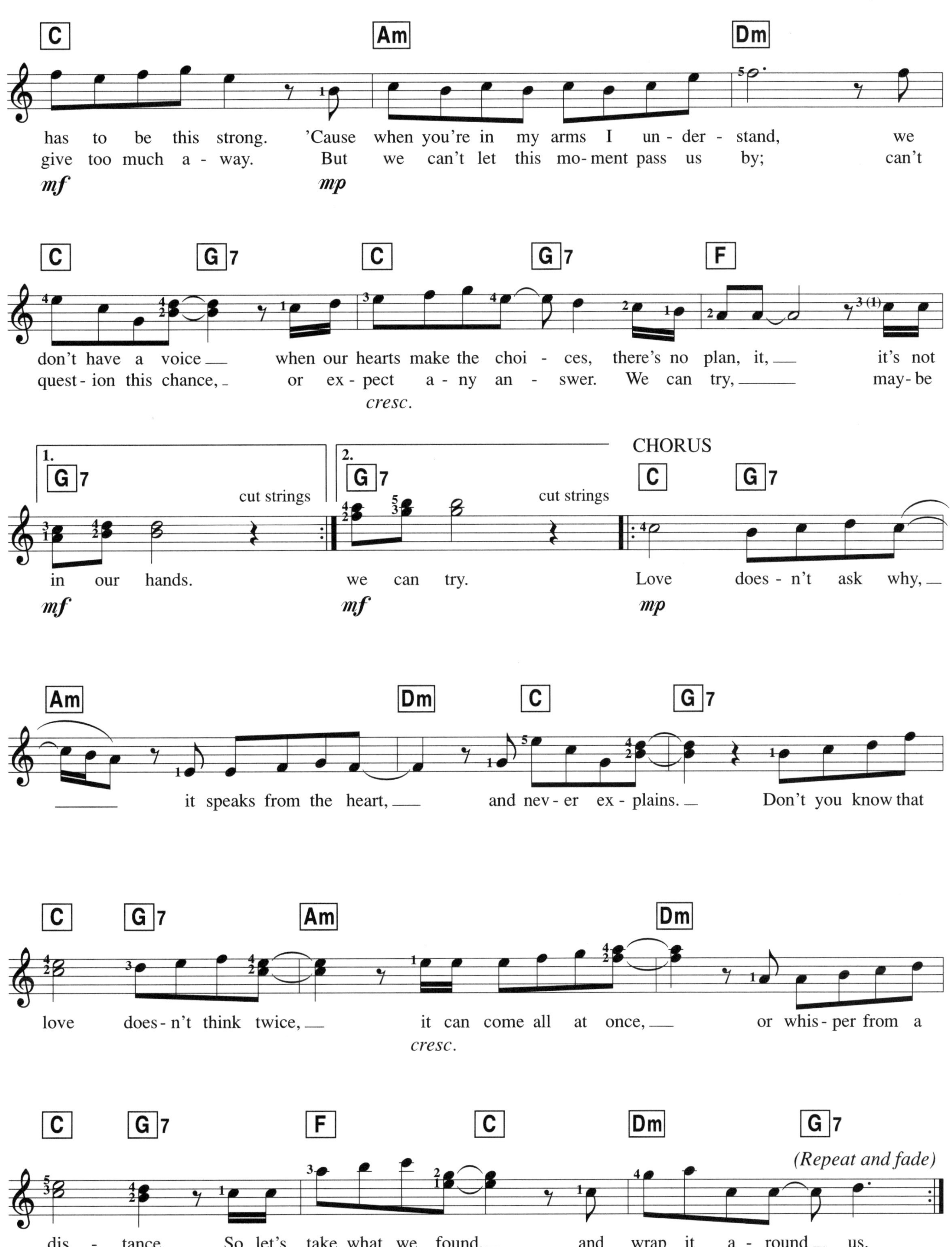
C Am Dm
has to be this strong. 'Cause when you're in my arms I un - der - stand, we
give too much a - way. But we can't let this mo- ment pass us by; can't
mf
mp
C G7 C G7 F
don't have a voice when our hearts make the choi - ces, there's no plan, it, it's not
quest- ion this chance, or ex - pect a - ny an - swer. We can try, may- be
cresc.
1.
2.
G7
cut strings
CHORUS
C G7
in our hands.
we can try.
Love does - n't ask why,
mf
mf
mp
Am Dm C G7
it speaks from the heart, and nev - er ex - plains. Don't you know that
C G7 Am Dm
love does - n't think twice, it can come all at once, or whis - per from a
cresc.
C G7 F C Dm G7
(Repeat and fade)
dis - tance. So let's take what we found, and wrap it a - round us.
mf

FALLING INTO YOU

Words & Music by Rick Nowles, Marie-Claire D'Ubalio & Billy Steinberg

Voice: clarinet
Rhythm: 8 beat
Tempo: medium (♩ = 96)

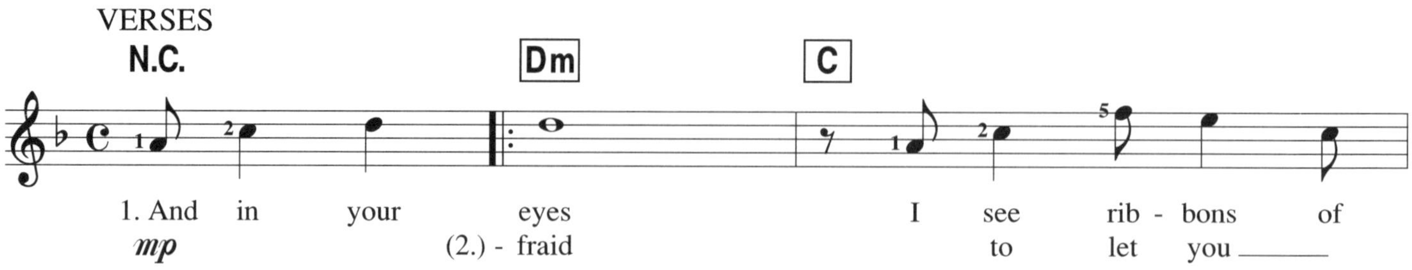

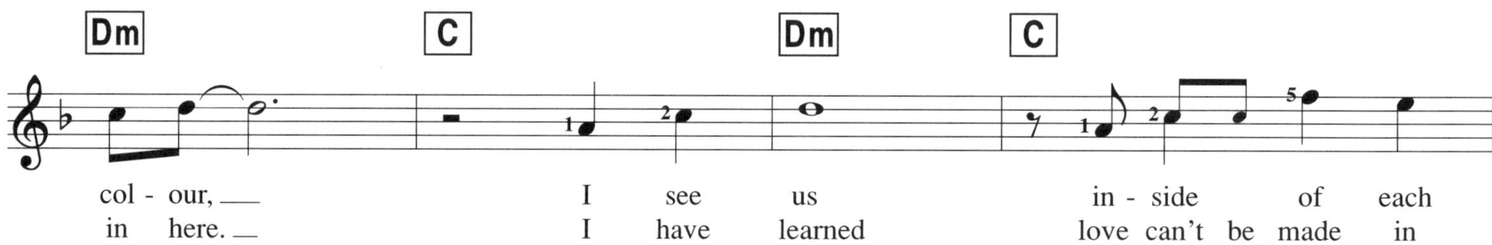

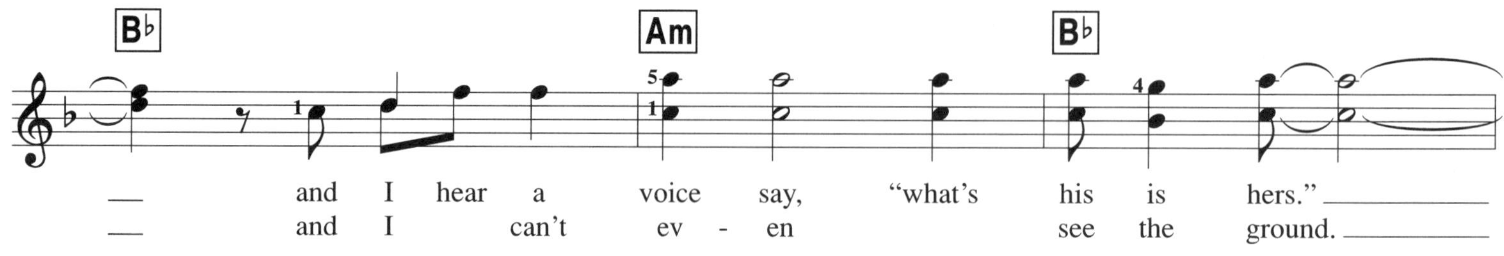

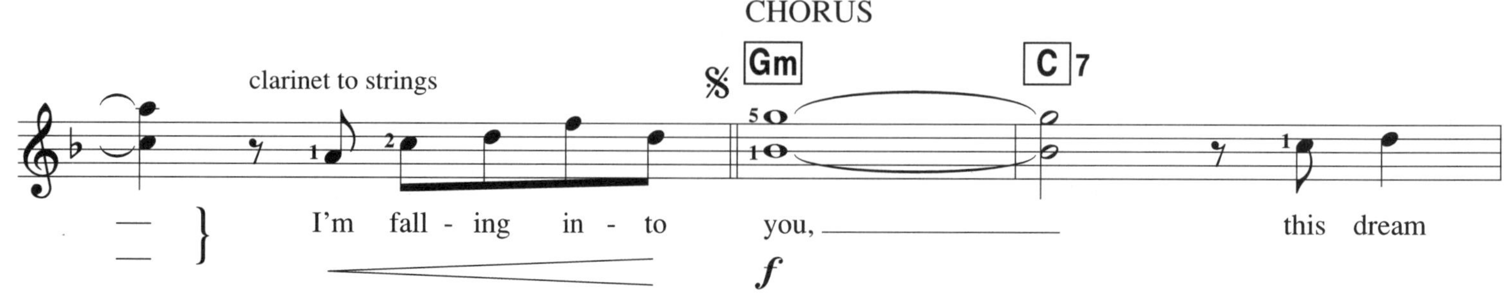

Gm
C7
Gm
C7
could come true.
And it feels so good,
fall - ing

1.
Dm
2.
Dm
strings to clarinet
in - to you.
2. I was a -
mp
in - to you.
Fall-ing like a leaf,

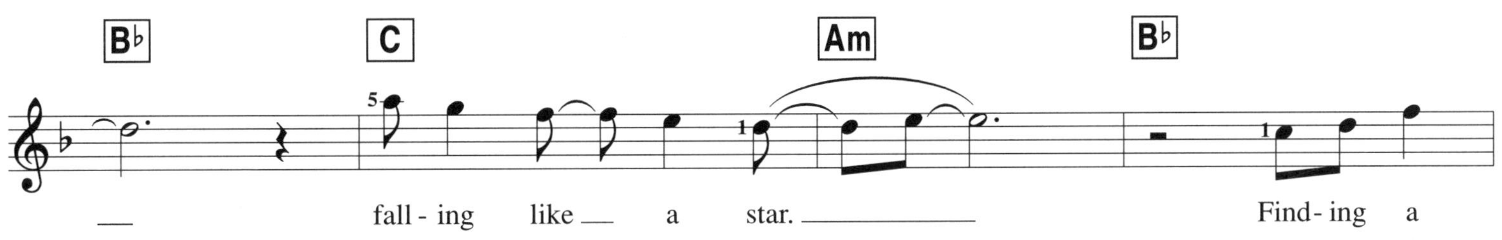
B♭
C
Am
B♭
fall - ing like a star.
Find - ing a

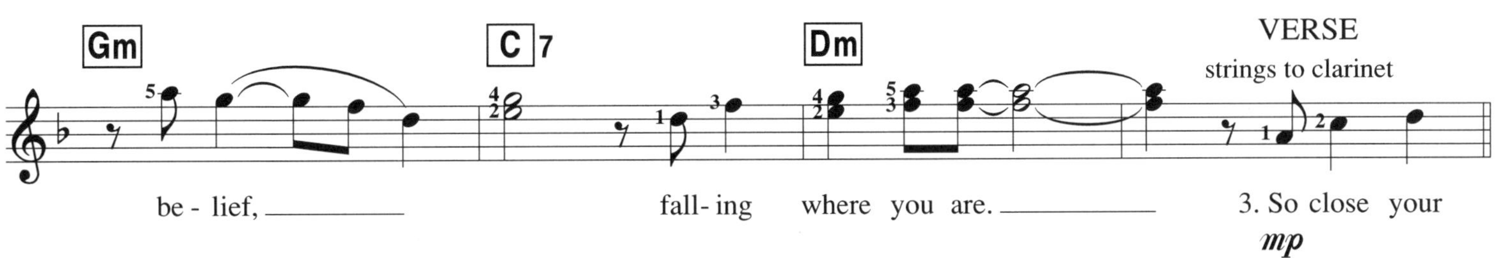
Gm
C7
Dm
VERSE
strings to clarinet
be - lief,
fall - ing where you are.
3. So close your
mp

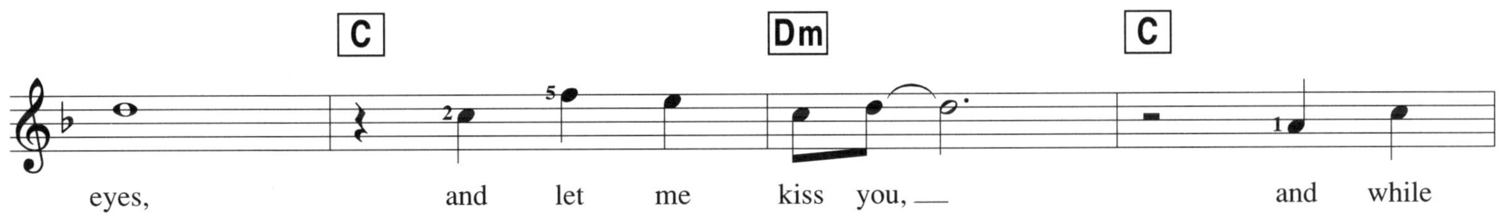
C
Dm
C
eyes,
and let me kiss you,
and while

D.%. (fade ad lib.)
Dm
C
Gm
C
clarinet to strings
you sleep.
I will miss you.
Oh, I'm fall - ing in - to

THE COLOUR OF MY LOVE

Words & Music by David Foster & Arthur Janov

Voice: oboe
Rhythm: 8 beat
Tempo: slow (♩ = 66)

G G7 C Am Bm Em
love. I'll paint the truth, show how I feel; try to make you com- plete- ly real; I'll use a

Am Bm C D7 G
brush so light and fine, to draw you close, and make you mine. I'll paint a
mp

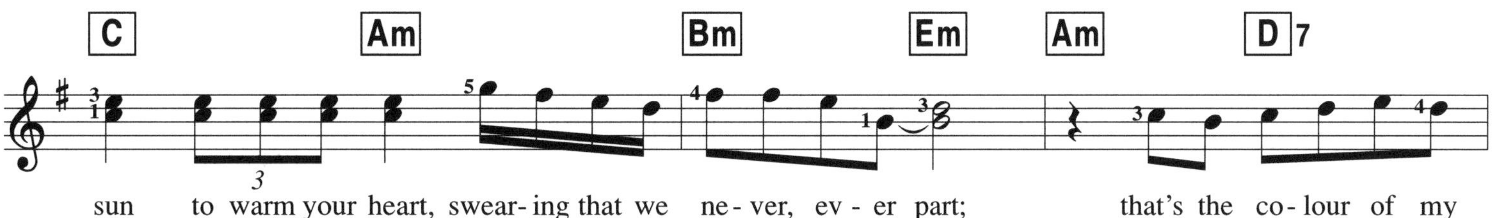
C Am Bm Em Am D7
sun to warm your heart, swear- ing that we ne- ver, ev - er part; that's the co- lour of my

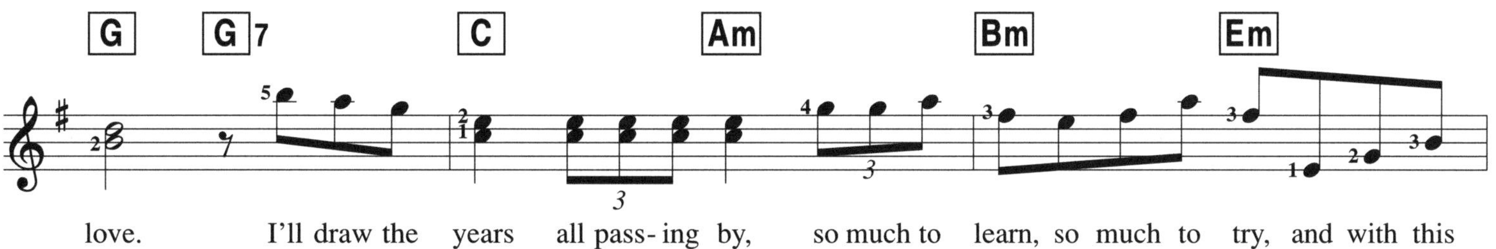
G G7 C Am Bm Em
love. I'll draw the years all pass- ing by, so much to learn, so much to try, and with this
cresc.

Am Bm Am Bm Am Bm
ring our lives will start, swear- ing that we'll ne- ver part; I of- fer what you can- not buy, de -
mf cresc.

C D7 G C Cm G
molto rit.
- vo - ted love un - til we die.
f stop rhythm

IMMORTALITY

Words & Music by Barry Gibb, Robin Gibb & Maurice Gibb

Voice: vibraphone
Rhythm: 8 beat
Tempo: medium (♩ = 88)

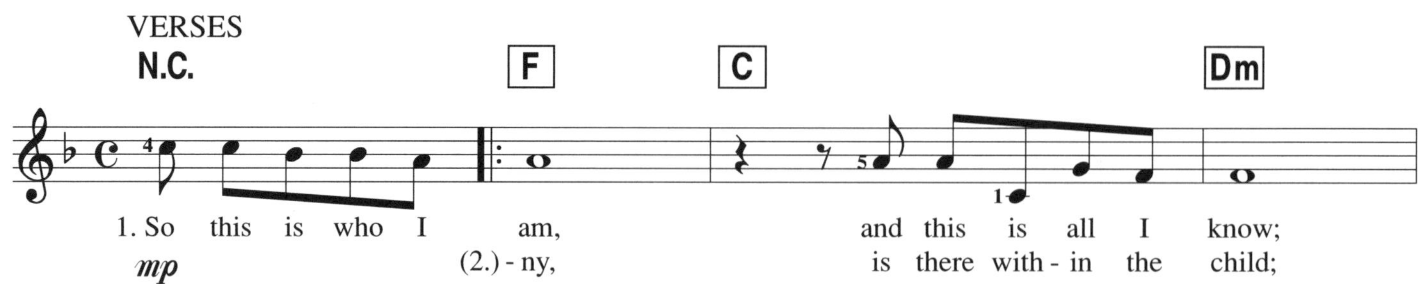

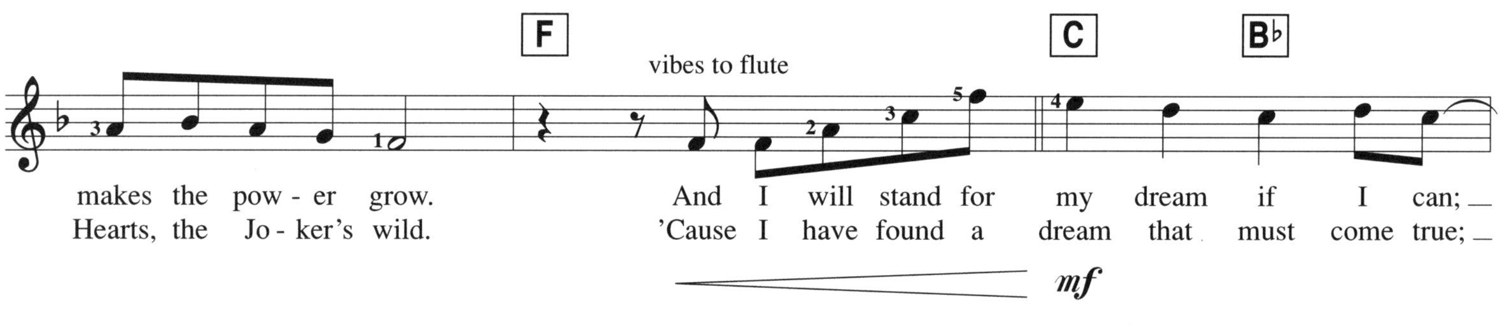

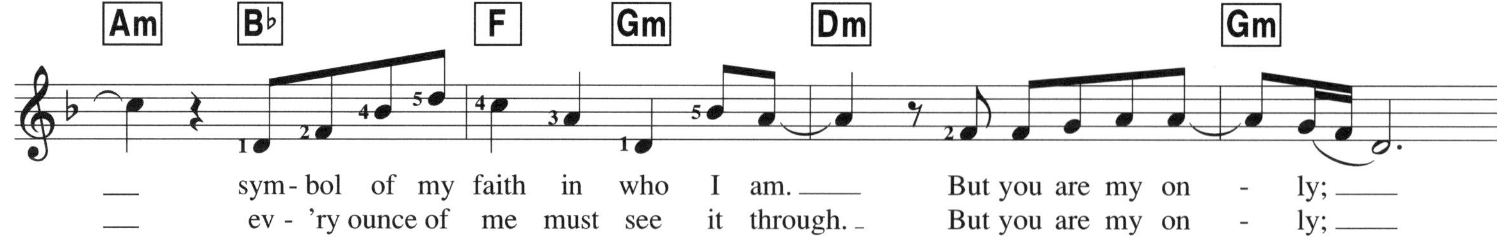

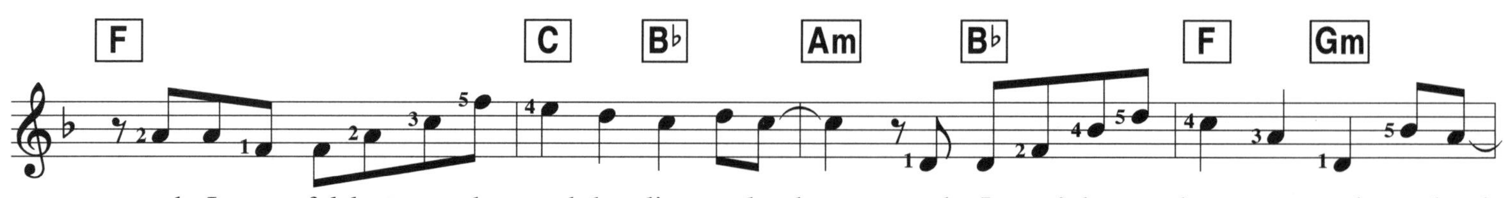

Dm Gm F
CHORUS
flute to vibes
but you are my on - ly.
and I will make them give to me.
And we don't say good - bye,
f
C Dm G Gm
we don't say good - bye.
And I know what I've got to be.
C F Gm Am Gm F Gm
add flute
Im - mor - ta - li - ty,
Im - mor - ta - li - ty,
mp
I make my jour - ney thro' e -
there is a vi - sion, and a
Am Gm F Gm Am Gm
- ter - ni - ty.
fire in me.
I keep the me - mo - ry of you and me in - side.
I keep the me - mo - ry of you and me in - side.
cresc.
mf
1. C (VERSE)
cut flute
2. Ful - fill your des - ti -
mp
2. C F C
And we don't say good - bye,
f
we don't say good -
Dm G Gm C F
(Repeat and fade)
- bye.
With all my love for you,
and what else we may do.
And we don't say good -

I'M YOUR ANGEL

Words & Music by R. Kelly

Voice: human voice
Rhythm: 8 beat
Tempo: slow (♩ = 56)

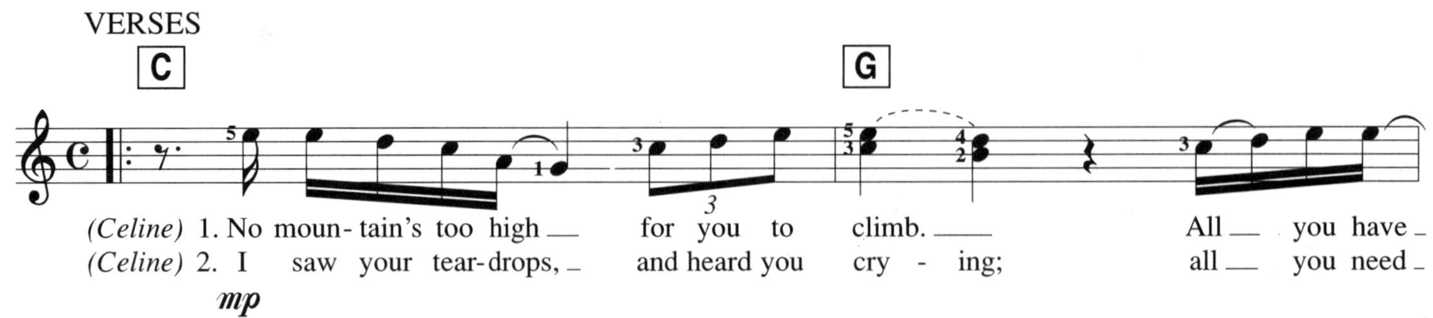

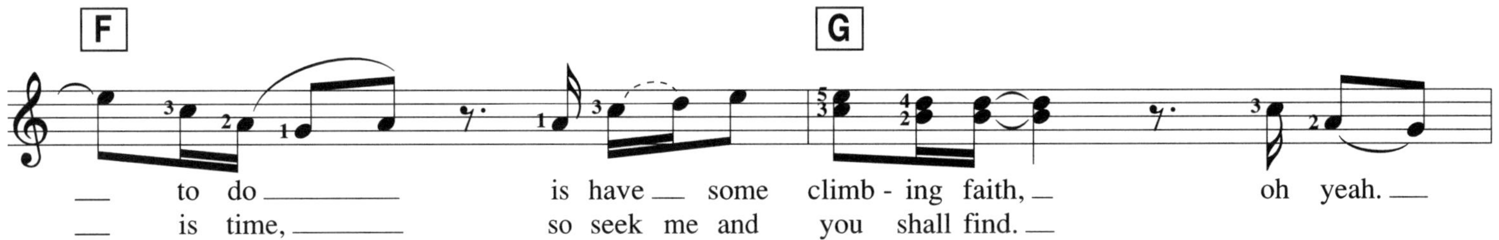

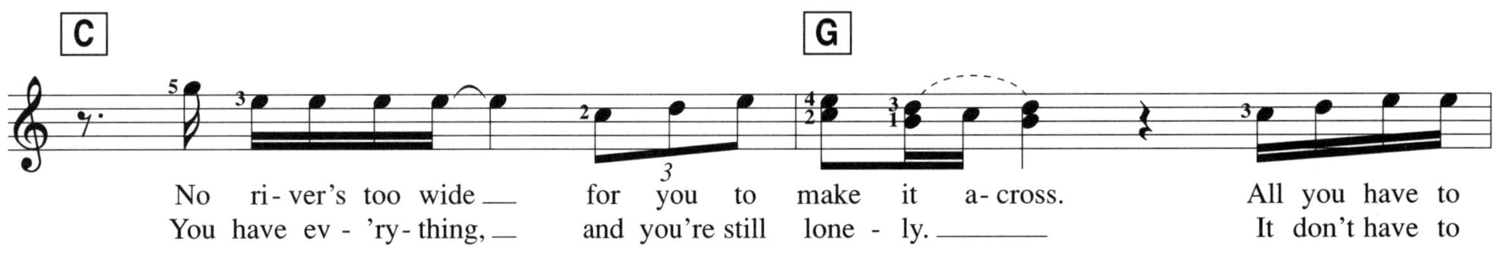

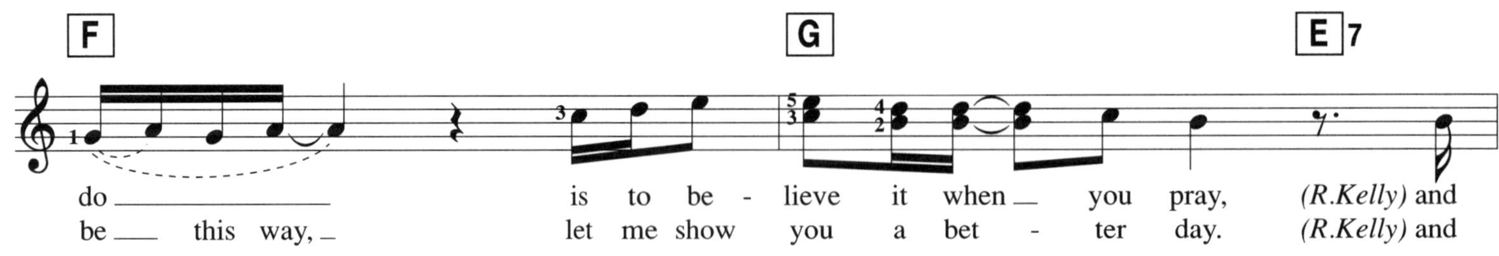

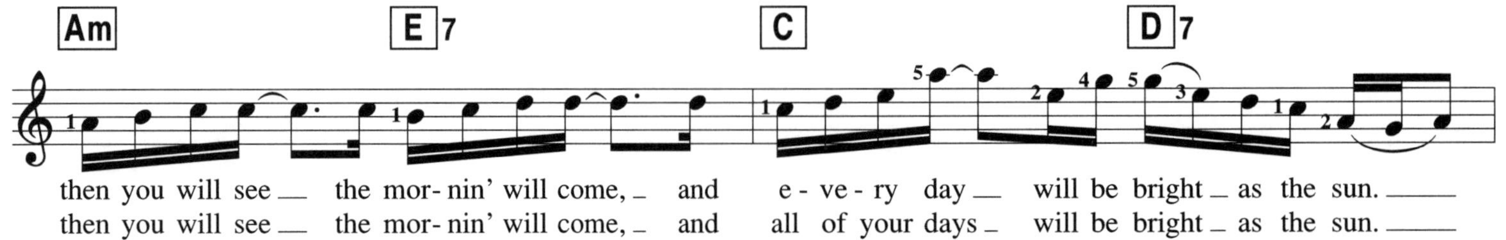

Dm
G
add strings
All of your fears, cast them on me. I just want you to see.
All of your fears, cast them on me. How can I make you see?
(Both) I'll be your
cresc.
f

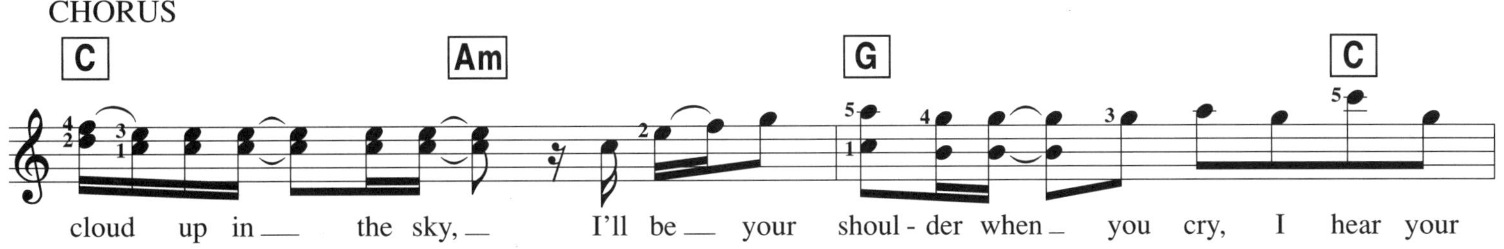
CHORUS
C
Am
G
C
cloud up in the sky, I'll be your shoul - der when you cry, I hear your

F
G
voi - ces when you call me, I am your an - gel. And when all

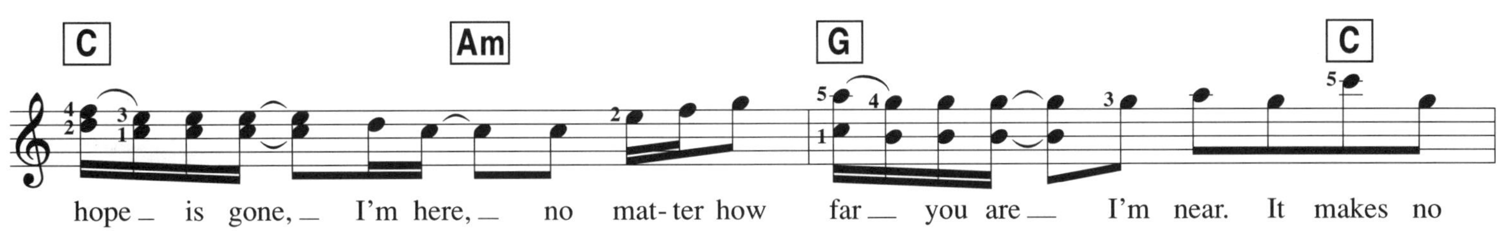
C
Am
G
C
hope is gone, I'm here, no mat - ter how far you are I'm near. It makes no

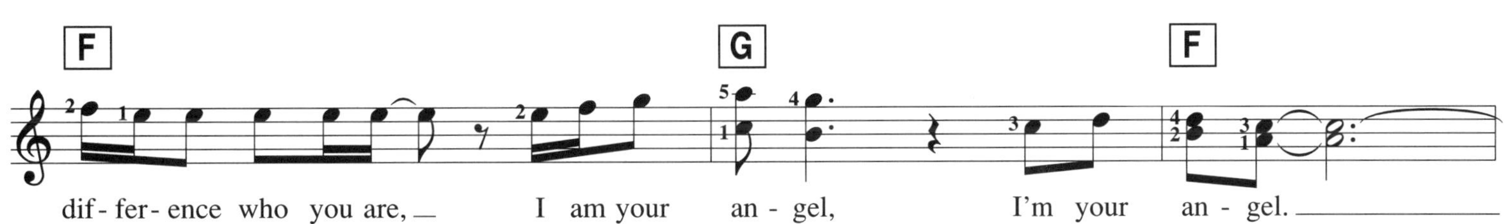
F
G
F
dif - fer - ence who you are, I am your an - gel, I'm your an - gel.

1.
2. BRIDGE
C
cut strings
C
F
Em
Dm
(R.Kelly) And when it's time to face the storm, (Celine) I'll be right by your side.
mp

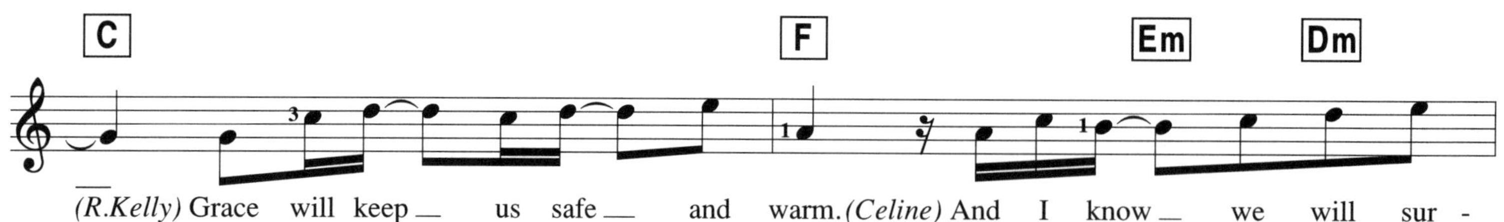
C F Em Dm
(R.Kelly) Grace will keep _ us safe _ and warm. (Celine) And I know _ we will sur -

Am E7 C D7 F
- vive. And when it seems _ as if _ your end _ is draw - ing near, _ don't you ev - er give up _ the fight. _ Put your
cresc.

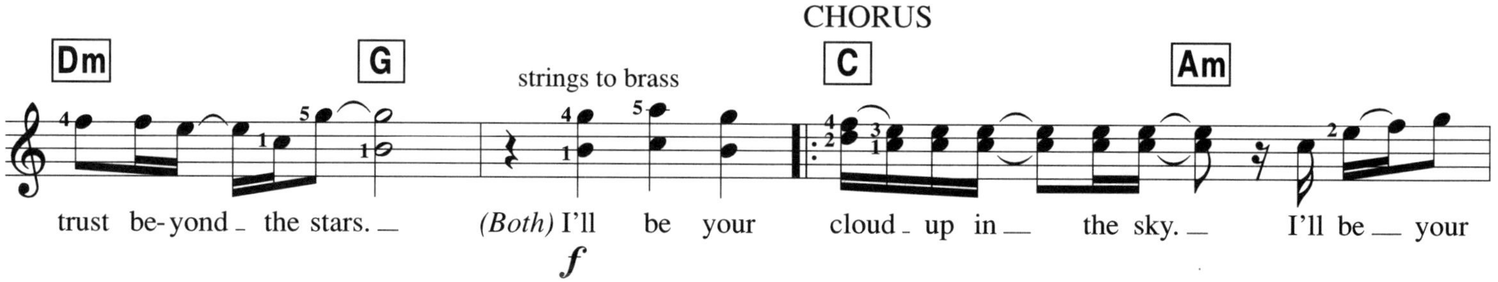
CHORUS
strings to brass
Dm G C Am
trust be - yond _ the stars. _ (Both) I'll be your cloud _ up in _ the sky. _ I'll be _ your
f

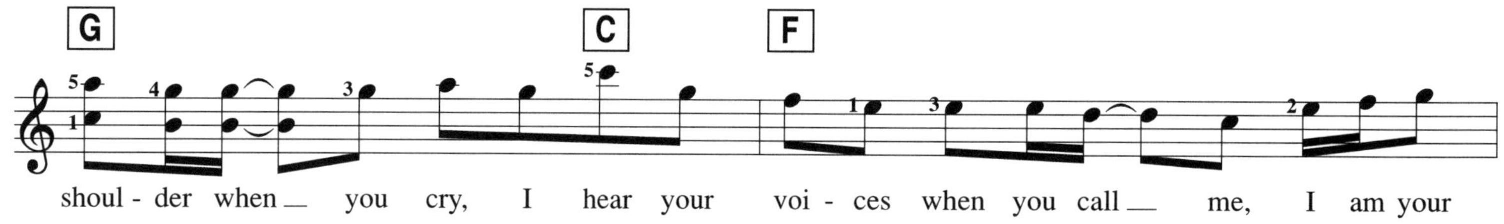
G C F
shoul - der when _ you cry, I hear your voi - ces when you call _ me, I am your

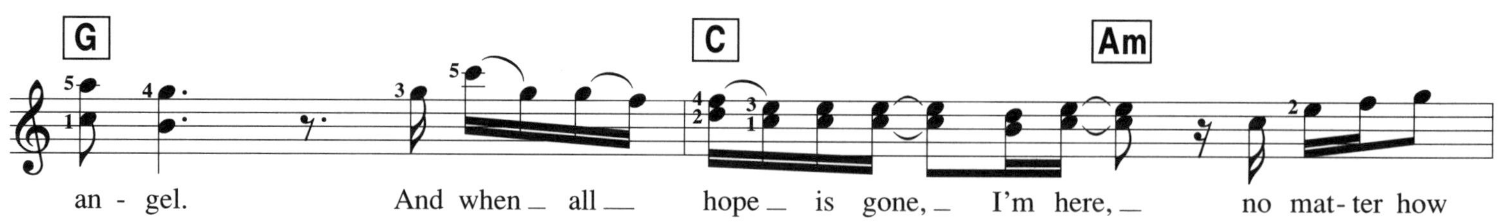
G C Am
an - gel. And when _ all _ hope _ is gone, _ I'm here, _ no mat - ter how

G C F G
(Repeat and fade)
far _ you are, _ I'm near, it makes no dif - fer - ence who you are, _ I am your an - gel. I'll be _ your _

CHORD CHARTS (For Left Hand)

C

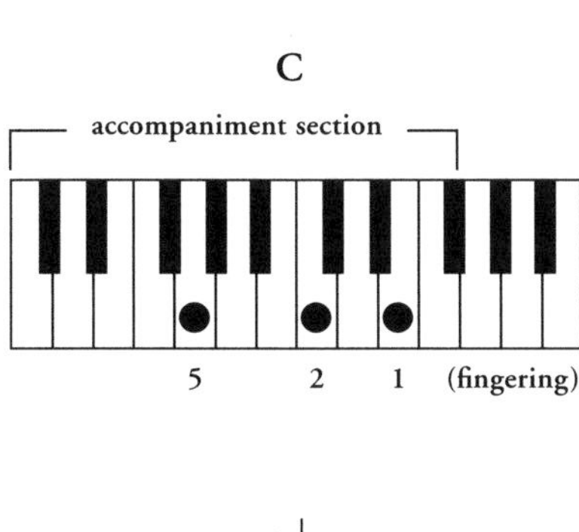

Cm

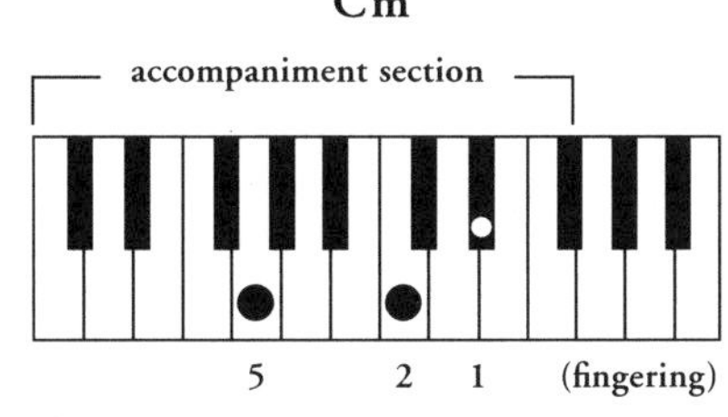

C7

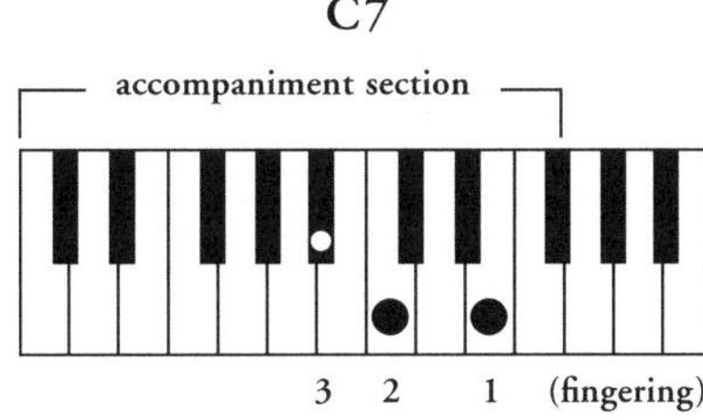

D♭

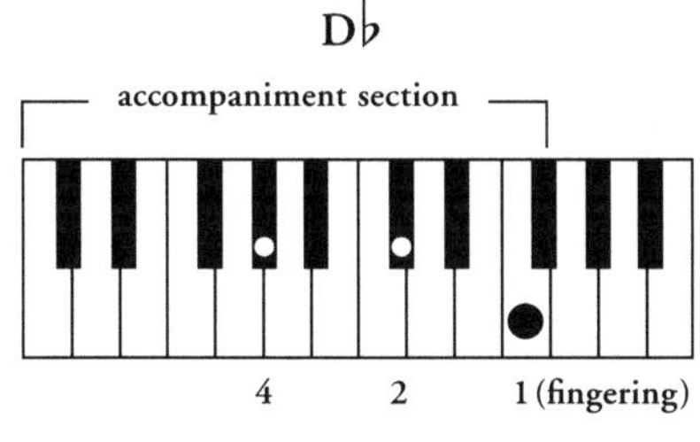

C♯m

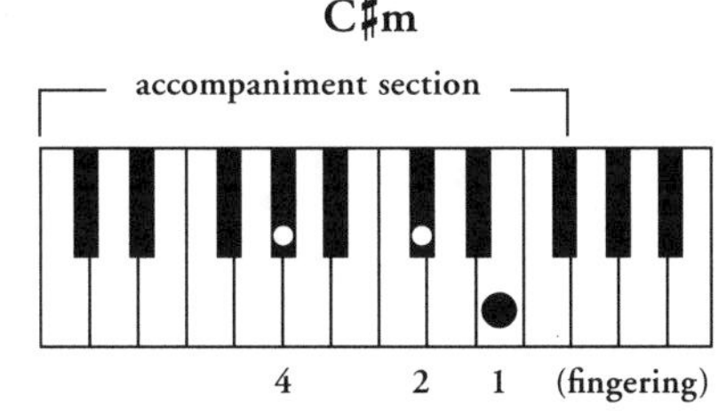

D♭(C♯)7

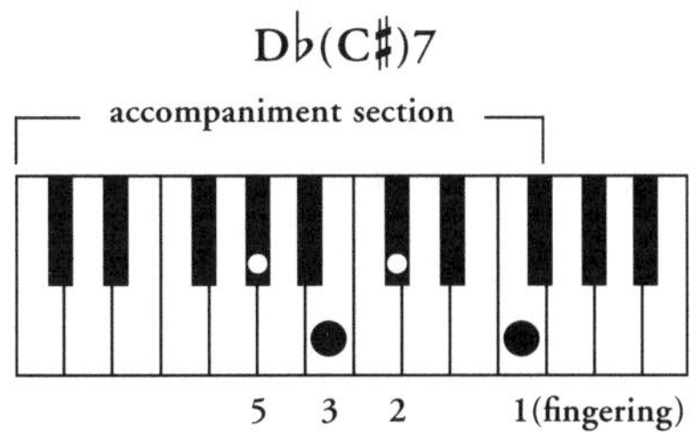

D

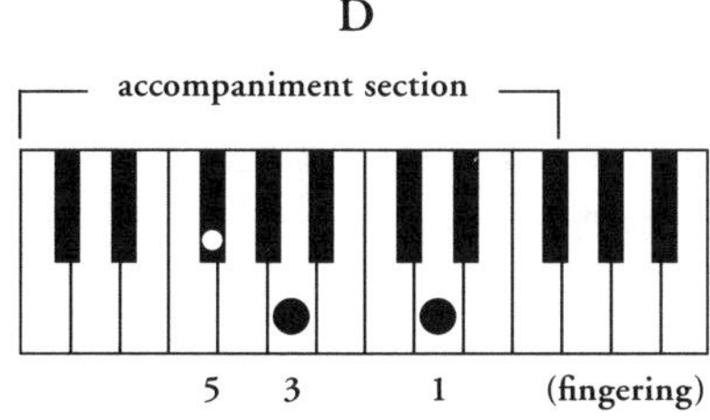

Dm

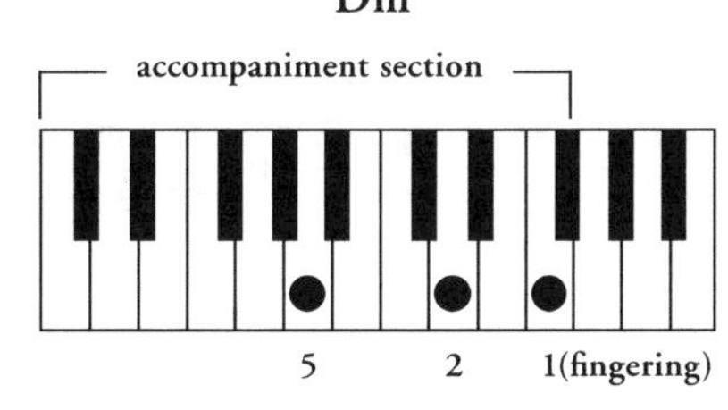

D7

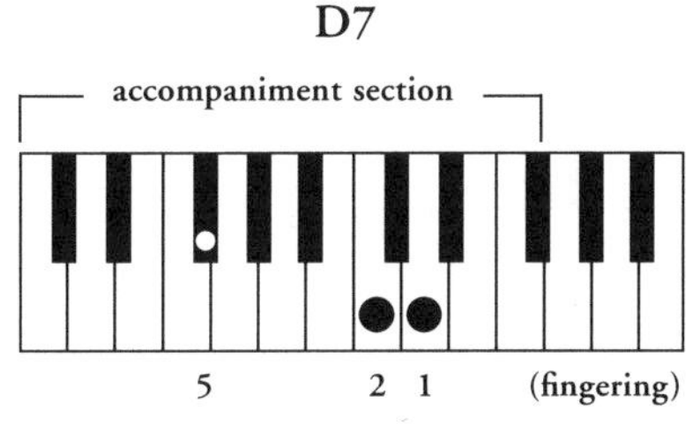

E♭

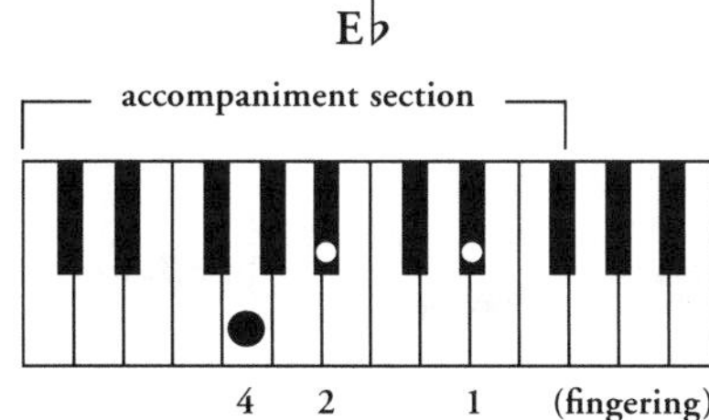

E♭m

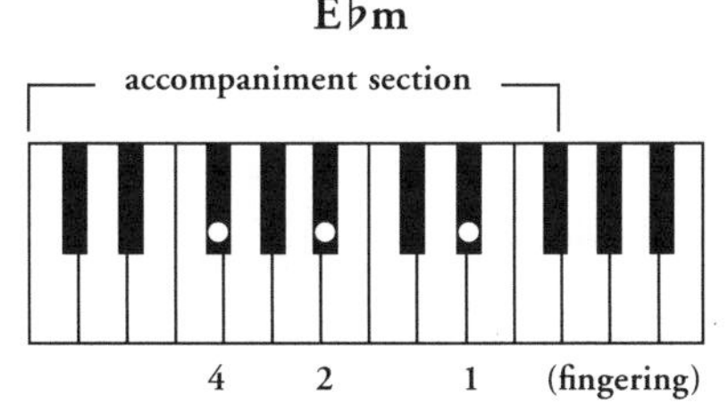

E♭7

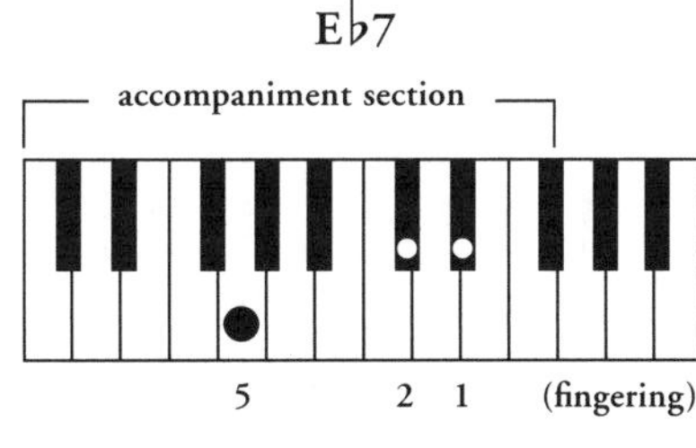

E

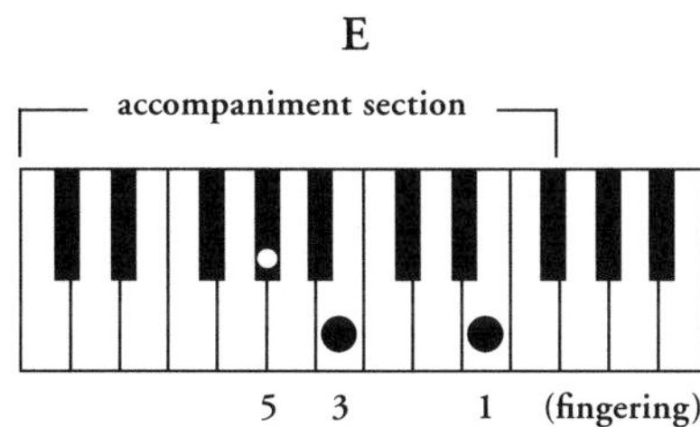

Em

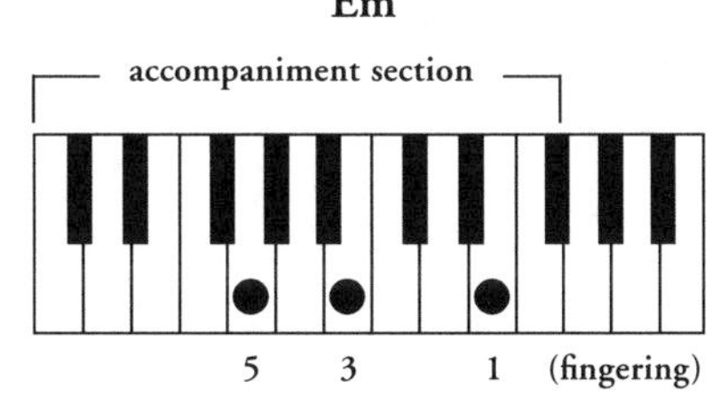

E7

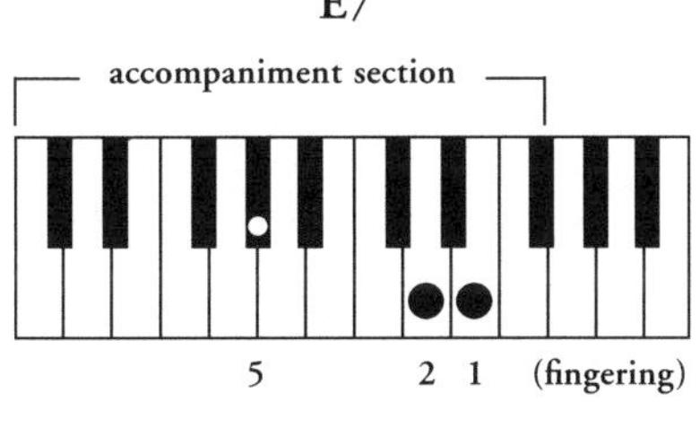

F

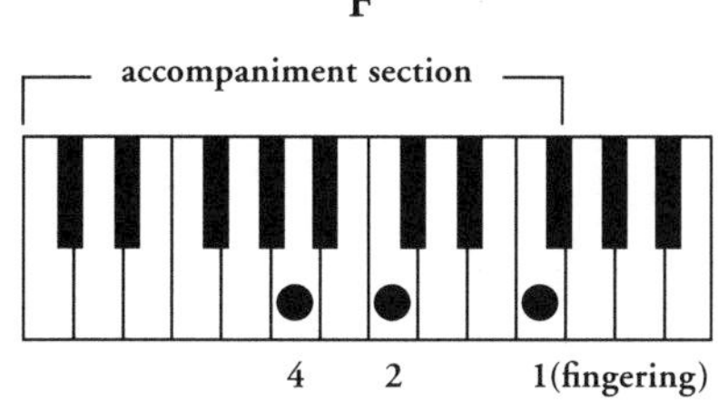

Fm

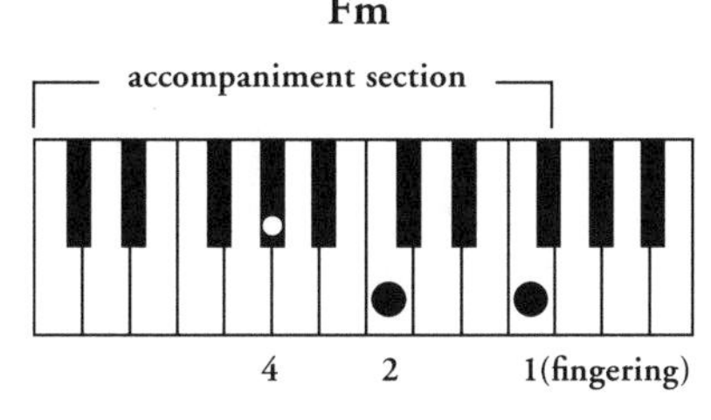

F7

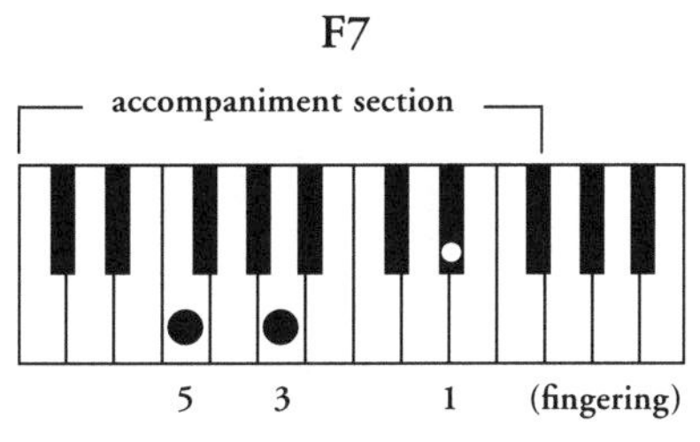

CHORD CHARTS (For Left Hand)

G♭(F♯)

accompaniment section

5 3 1 (fingering)

F♯m

accompaniment section

5 3 1 (fingering)

G♭(F♯)7

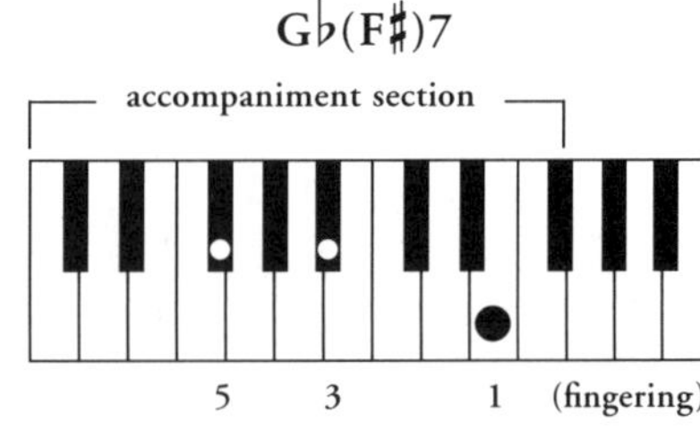

G

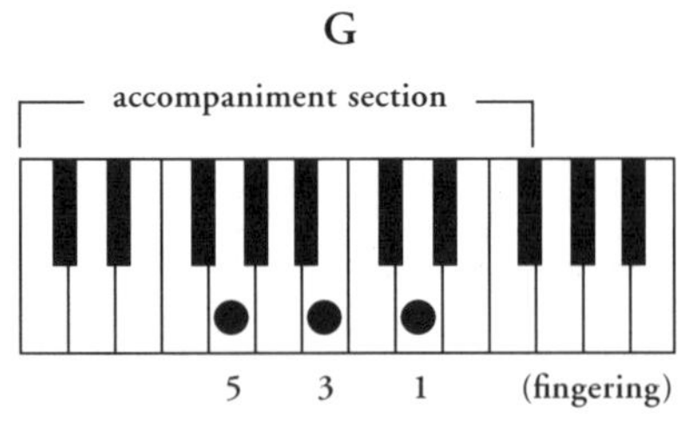

Gm

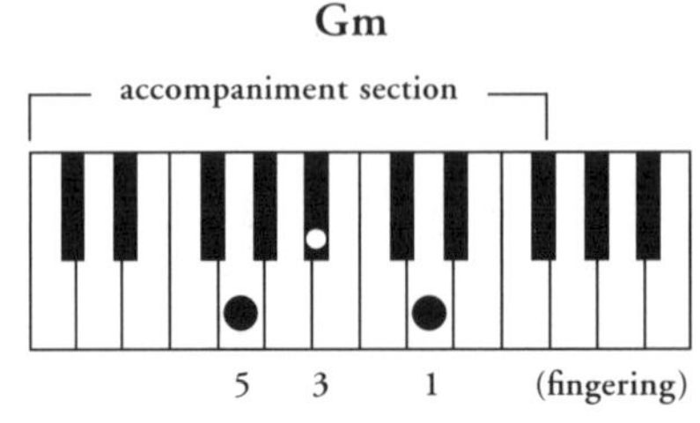

G7

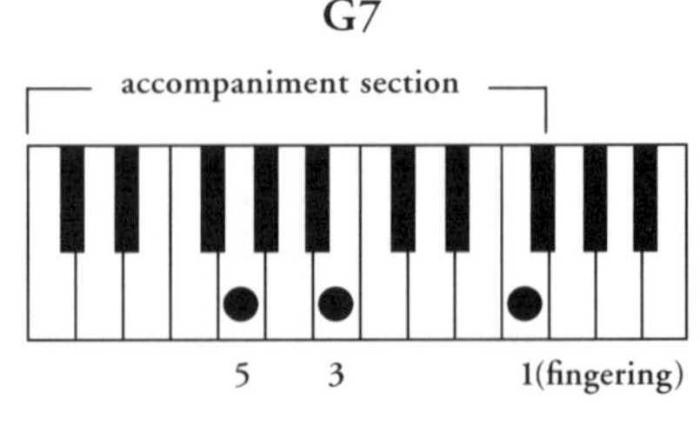

A♭

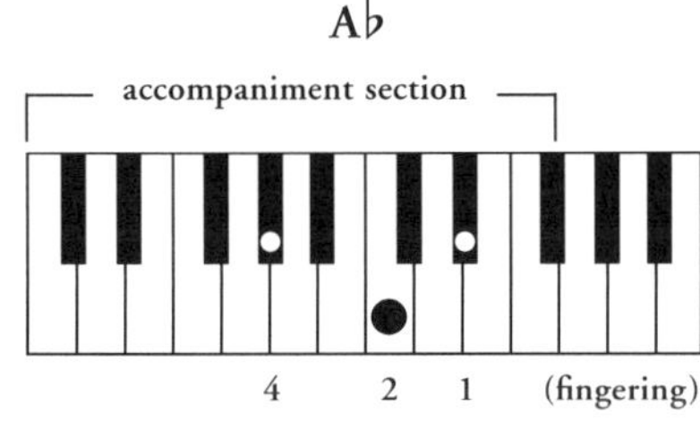

A♭m

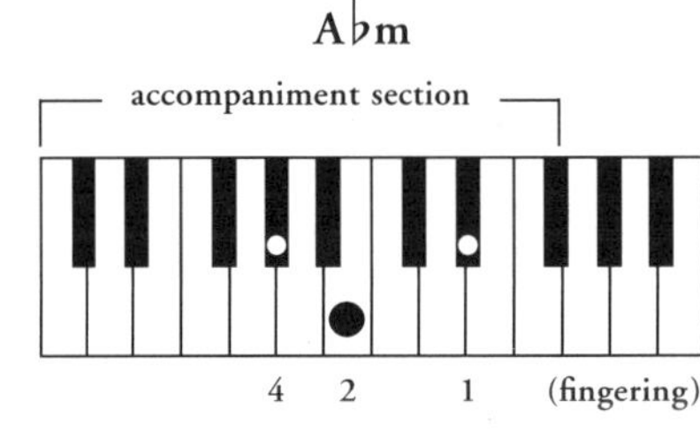

A♭7

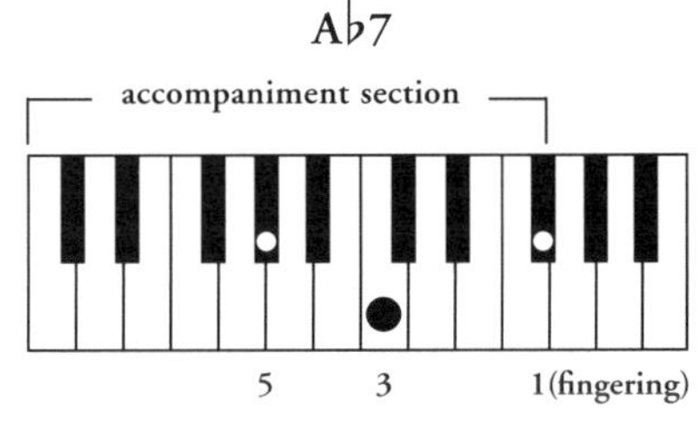

A

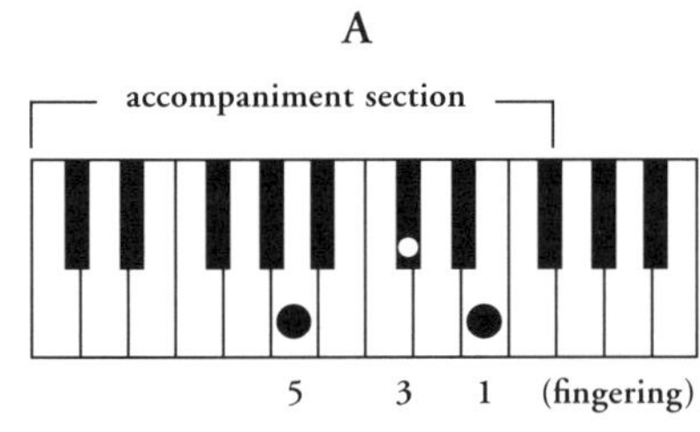

Am

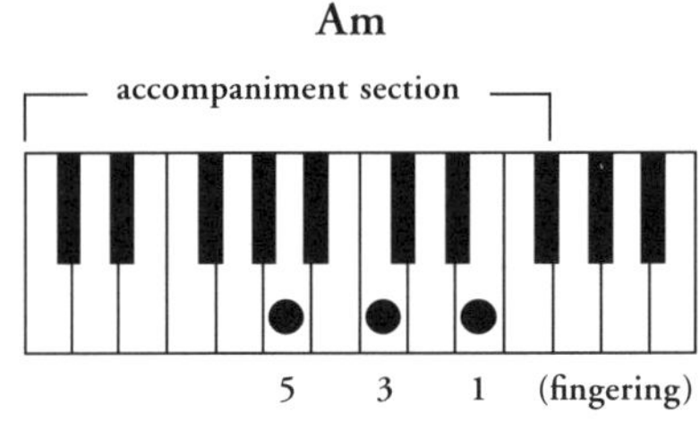

A7

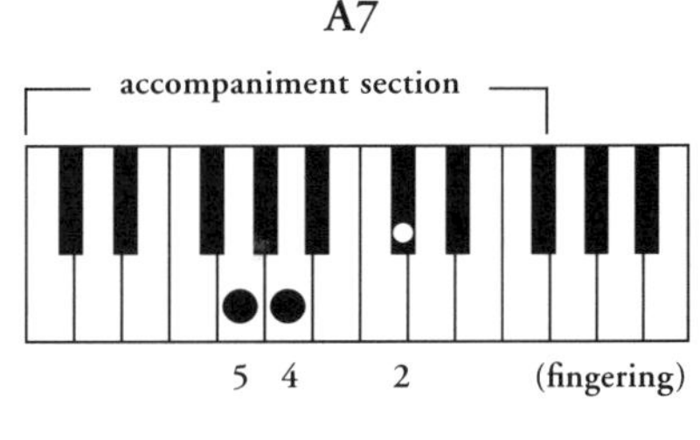

B♭

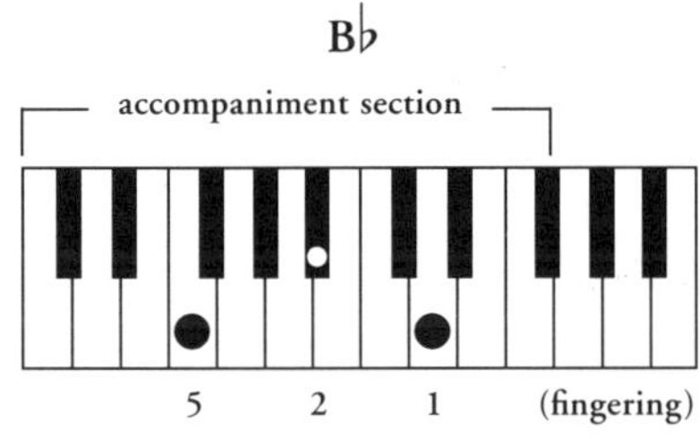

B♭m

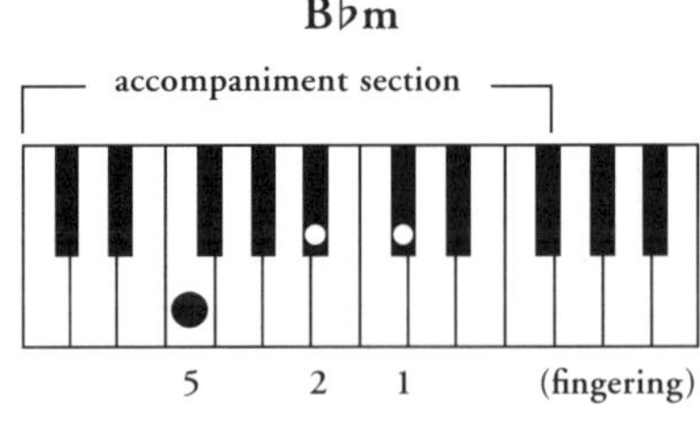

B♭7

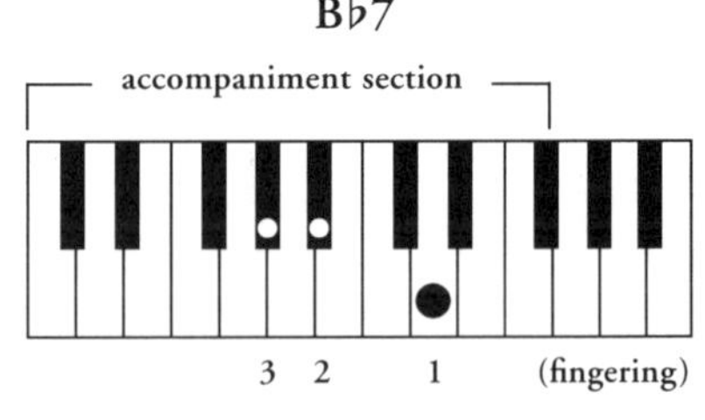

B

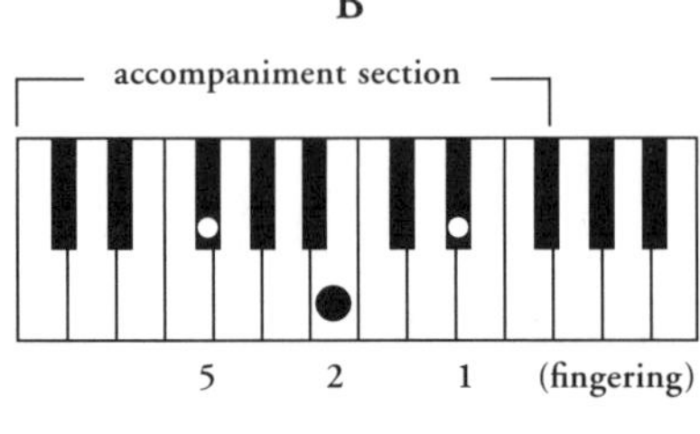

Bm

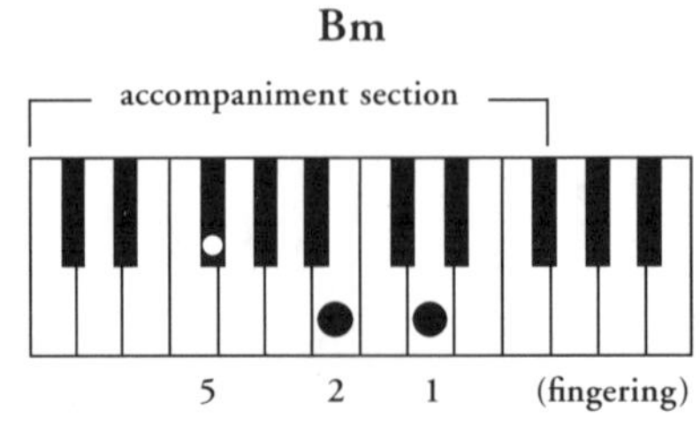

B7

accompaniment section

4 3 2 (fingering)